Running into Happiness

Running into Happiness

How my happiness habit journal created lasting
happiness in the midst of a crazy-busy semester

ANGELICA RIBEIRO

ISBN: 1983745790
ISBN 13: 9781983745799
Library of Congress Control Number: 2018900788
CreateSpace Independent Publishing Platform
North Charleston, South Carolina

To Grandma Margarida,
who has inspired me with her genuine kindness, positivity, and happiness

Contents

Acknowledgments

To be honest, I usually don't read the acknowledgments section of books. But as I sit to write these acknowledgments, I realize that, to me, this section is as important as the rest of the book. I say that because I wouldn't have published this book if it weren't for all the people who helped me throughout the process of writing it.

I appreciate all the support I received from family members and friends such as Diana Alves and Juan Manuel Martin. Certain people played particularly important roles during the process of writing this book.

Thanks to Wladmir Pacheco for his friendship and for going on that walk with me, when my new-me journey started.

Thanks to Mary Richardson for reading and giving me feedback on the first drafts and encouraging and supporting me with this book, even when it was just an idea.

Thanks to Uncle Francisco Fontelene for his words of wisdom, encouragement, and patience for reading the draft of this book using Google Translator.

Thanks to my early readers who commented on drafts: James D. Moss, Joy Moss, Amanda Franks, Patricia Goodson, Edith Cassell, Melika Shirmohammadi, Tana Divoll, Isabel Oliveira, Daniel Giffoni,

Tania Ramos, Marina Sanchez, and Laura Quisenberry. Their feedback certainly enhanced this book.

Thanks to Val Nelson for exchanging ideas on happiness and helping me come up with the name My Happiness Habit Journal.

I also want to thank Isabel Ferreira, Aunt Margareth Fontenele, Socorro Silva, Isabel Oliveira, Sharitza Ordonez, Michiko Fuji, and Melika Shirmohammadi for applying My Happiness Habit Journal. Their input on their personal experiences with the journal meant a lot to me.

Huge thanks to Stephanie Campbell, who helped me edit the book.

Thanks to my parents and God for allowing me to share my happiness journey with you.

Thanks to you, Kent, for sharing your life with me. My happiness wouldn't be complete without you. I love you!

Setting the Stage

I decided to write this book on how I ran into happiness to share the possible effects that happy feelings can bring to your life. The same way happiness greatly impacted my life, it can also positively impact yours. Happiness made me feel empowered to face challenges, taught me to find meaning in different everyday situations, and allowed me to get to know myself better. Moreover, happiness increased my assertiveness as I stood up for my own values and beliefs.

This book is for everyone who has the feeling of living in a maze, trying to find the path to happiness. As scientist and author Steven Hayes suggests, our culture tends to make us believe in shortcuts for happiness, such as going to a party, buying a new car, or being accepted into a university.[1] These shortcuts, without a doubt, bring us happy feelings, but not long-lasting happiness. Unfortunately, the path to long-lasting happiness is still unknown to many people. Perhaps many people haven't experienced long-term happiness because they try to *find* the path to happiness, instead of trying to *create* the path to happiness, as Sonja Lyubomirsky, the author of *The How of Happiness*, suggests.

I am an ordinary person you would see buying groceries at a store, exercising at a gym, or paying the mortgage at a bank. I am

---

1. Hayes, "Empty Promise."

not a best-selling book author. But as a PhD student, I am a professional writer. I started seeing myself as a writer after reading the book *Becoming an Academic Writer*, by Patricia Goodson, a professor at Texas A&M University. Goodson says that graduate students and professors are professional writers: We write for a living because everything we do requires writing. We write papers, journal articles, book chapters, research grants, reports, and reviews. Since my plan is to be a professor, this is just the beginning of my life as a writer. With that said, I decided to use my writing skills to share with you how I ran into happiness in the midst of a very busy academic semester.

This book tells the story of what started as *my new-me journey* and ended as *my happiness journey*. Even though I have always been a very determined, goal-oriented person who wanted to grow professionally, I was pessimistic, which was probably due to a lack of self-esteem, confidence, and feeling of being valued. In the beginning, I called this journey *my new me* because I wanted to improve myself as a person but didn't know exactly what to look for in order to improve myself. So whatever it was, my new me would capture it (if I actually improved something about me; otherwise, it would just be called *the still-me journey*). However, my new-me journey made me realize I was looking for happiness. Therefore, I changed the name of my journey to my happiness journey, inspired by Gretchen Rubin through her book *The Happiness Project*. As a result, my happiness journey took me beyond making me a happier person—it also made me an optimistic, confident, and assertive person.

Being able to create lasting happiness was one of the main lessons I learned during my happiness journey. Therefore, besides sharing how I ran into happiness, this book shares *My Happiness Habit Journal*, a tool I designed based on the works of experts and authors on happiness. My

Happiness Habit Journal helped me create lasting happiness and can help you create yours too.

Anyone who wants to be happier can benefit from my experience, including undergraduate students and stay-at-home or working parents who have hectic lives. However, I believe that this book can especially benefit graduate students. Being a doctoral student myself while writing this book, I understand the challenges graduate students go through.

An acceptance letter to a graduate program brings a lot of joy, but it also comes with challenging moments. Doctoral programs, for example, not only prepare us, PhD students, to be experts in our fields but also train us to accomplish many things in a short period of time. For instance, we learn to read hundreds of pages per week, write a paper in one day, quickly think of arguments in favor or against a certain topic, question what we read or hear, find solutions for our own problems, and look for answers for what we don't know. Moreover, doctoral programs expect us to attend and present at conferences, publish articles, participate in projects with professors, and, of course, do well in our coursework. If we are not careful, meeting doctoral programs' high expectations can lead us to lonely and unhappy personal lives. Although we can be successful and happy with our performance and accomplishments in our academic lives, we may not be fully happy in our personal lives. The amount of time that we have to devote to our studies may draw us away from our families and friends. The dedication to our academic lives may lead us to a stressful personal life because we don't make time to rest or have fun with our loved ones. Graduate programs do not come with a manual to teach us how to balance our academic and personal lives. We are responsible to learn on our own how to balance the two, and unfortunately, many graduate students are never able to find this elusive balance. Here's an example that illustrates the lack of balance between academic and personal lives. Not too long ago, I heard someone asking a graduate student, who was sitting by himself, "Where are your friends?"

"Friends? I'm a graduate student. I don't have any friends," the student replied with conviction.

My experience in finding long-lasting happiness was guided by various works of authors and researchers on happiness and positive psychology. Although my experiences might differ from yours, I hope this book inspires you to create your own path to long-lasting happiness, especially if you are a busy graduate student. In order to make this book more meaningful to you, at the end of the chapters, I ask you questions as a way to encourage you to apply what I have learned throughout my new-me journey and my happiness journey. I want you, too, to have and use the tools and knowledge that led me to my lasting happiness.

I hope you enjoy my happiness journey. Before diving into how I ran into happiness, let me introduce myself.

Angelica

I am a doctoral student at Texas A&M University, in College Station, Texas. Here's how I got to this point in my life. I was born and raised in Fortaleza, Brazil. As I was turning fifteen years old, I was presented with two birthday-gift choices: (1) a big fancy birthday party or (2) a fifteen-day trip to Disney World. My parents, who value education and personal growth, gave me a third choice: one year in the United States as an exchange student. Since my values are similar to my parents', I chose to be away from the comfort of my home and the support and love of my family and friends to live in the United States for a year, something I had never thought about doing.

It was the first time I had ever left my family and the surroundings I called home. I knew it was not going to be easy, facing many linguistic and cultural challenges, not to mention having to compete at the same academic level with students who were born and raised in the United States. However, that did not stop me; instead, I focused on all I could learn, while sharing what I knew. I trusted the values and principles that my parents had instilled in me, and because they believed in me, I knew I would overcome all the obstacles I was about to face. And I was right.

The 1994–95 academic year was challenging, because I started it by living with a host family who was unknown to me, having no friends, and speaking very little English. However, my determination to succeed academically and to be able to solve my own problems independently helped me turn that challenging year into a successful one. This enriching experience was a turning point in my life and determined the career I would enter. At the end of the year, I was proficient in English, my name was listed on the honor roll at school, and I had developed many problem-solving skills. For example, when I was failing history because of my low English proficiency, I decided to audio-record my classes and ask my host mother to listen to and explain them to me. Although she didn't speak Portuguese, she was able to explain the content in a way I could understand. I can definitely say that as a result of my exchange-student experience, I became a more confident, disciplined, and mature person.

The academic year I spent in the United States also made me humble because I realized that there was much more to learn. Although I did not know it then, the exchange-student experience was the initiation into my teaching career and passion I have for education. During my college career in Brazil, I started working as an English teacher and researching in the field of learning a second language. I was fortunate to meet Professor Manolisa Vasconcellos, who was the first person to inspire me to do research. We conducted a research study to identify common English pronunciation errors that preservice teachers from Brazil usually make. For example, since the Portuguese language doesn't have the sounds represented by the letters *th*, when learning English, Brazilians tend to replace them with *d* or *t* sounds. My work with Vasconcellos opened a thirst for learning and a delightful intellectual curiosity unknown to me.

As a result, I returned to the United States to pursue my master's degree in bilingual/ESL (English as a second language) education at the University of Massachusetts Amherst. I chose a university in Massachusetts to be close to friends I had made during my exchange-student experience. I had the pleasure of taking classes under excellent professors, including Sonia Nieto and Theresa Austin, who played a major role in my academic life. Austin increased my desire to learn and taught me how to be a critical thinker, especially when conducting research.

My original plan was to go back to Brazil after two years, which was the time I needed to complete the master's program. However, I eventually decided to stay in the United States. My aunt Teresa had been right. In 2004, when my mother told her that I was coming to the United States to study, Aunt Teresa said, "Angelica is not coming back."

"Of course she is. She even has a boyfriend here," my mother said.

"It doesn't matter. You will see. Angelica will meet an American man, get married, and stay in the United States."

When I ran into Aunt Teresa that year, she told me the same thing. I smiled and said, "Aunt Teresa, I will definitely come back. I have no plans to stay there."

"That's what you say now," she said.

Well, although Aunt Teresa didn't believe me, my plan was, indeed, to return to Brazil. I could not even imagine myself not living there. That's why, whenever I went to Fortaleza on vacation during those two years, I would take everything I wasn't going to need in the United States any longer. That was true until my third semester of the master's program, when my future husband, Kent, and I started dating. By then, I had already broken up with my boyfriend in Brazil. After Kent and I started talking about getting married, he helped me bring all my things back to the United States.

Kent and I met in a classroom at the University of Massachusetts Amherst. He was a PhD student at the time and was taking one of his last credited courses, which happened to be one of my first courses in the program. About three years later, at our engagement party in Fortaleza, I heard Aunt Teresa saying to my mother, "See, I told you! Angelica is not coming back to Brazil." This time, my mother and I could not deny it. Since Kent didn't (and still doesn't) speak Portuguese, we didn't even consider living there.

In 2008, we married in Massachusetts, Kent's home state, and in 2009, we had our religious ceremony in Fortaleza. This way, both of our families had the chance to celebrate our wedding with us. Soon after we got married, we moved to Houston, Texas, where we currently live. Why Houston? Well, being from Fortaleza, a city where summer is the only season throughout the year, I told Kent that I would live in the United States, but not in a cold place like Massachusetts. It was fine to live there for a few years while I completed my master's program, but to be there for years and years to come would be too much. To my relief, he agreed to leave Massachusetts. Since he was looking for a job at that time, we made a list of possible states where we would like to live. In our list we had Florida, Texas, Hawaii, California, and South Carolina. After we made the list, he went online to find out where there were openings for a professor position. It didn't take long for him to find an opening at the University of Houston–Clear Lake. He applied, got the job, and here we are!

We've been living in Houston for ten years now. During five of those years, I worked in a middle school as an English-as-a-second-language teacher. I really enjoyed working with English-language learners, but at the same time, I wanted to grow in my teaching career and do something to improve their education. Therefore, I decided to quit my job and go back to school to earn a PhD in curriculum and instruction (with focus on English as a second language) so that I can become a professor and researcher in the field of education. As I write this, I am a third-year doctoral student who ran into happiness in the midst of an academic semester that didn't seem to have any room for it. This book chronicles that journey to happiness and shares my insights on how you, too, can achieve happiness, even as a graduate student.

One

LEARNING STRATEGIES FOR A BETTER LIFE

It was May of 2015. I was simply going for a walk with a good friend of mine, Wladmir, along Beira Mar Beach, one of the main tourist attractions of my hometown of Fortaleza, Brazil. I had no idea that our conversation would soon change my life. Here's what happened.

Wladmir and I have been friends for more than twenty-one years. Unfortunately, we rarely see each other now because I live in the United States and he lives in Brazil. However, we don't let the distance between us affect our friendship. It doesn't matter how often we see each other; we know that we can always count on one another. Whenever we get together, we have a lot to catch up on. So that year it was no different. As we went for a walk, I told him all about my first two years in the PhD program, and he told me about his job and future plans, including his wedding.

Wladmir works for Paulo Vieira, a Brazilian life coach who conducts workshops on emotional intelligence, among other topics. After listening to all the benefits of the emotional-intelligence workshops that Vieira conducts, I said to Wladmir, "I'd love to attend one of those workshops, but it's so expensive!"

"But you don't have to attend his workshop to learn the content, tools, and strategies that he teaches. You can find them on YouTube," Wladmir said. "There are several people who don't go to the workshops, just watch the YouTube videos, and say that their lives changed too. It's all about being committed to putting into practice the strategies that Paulo Vieira teaches and wanting to change something about you."

Being able to find Vieira's main workshop content for free was exactly what I wanted to hear. *If the strategies worked for those people, they would probably work for me, too, because I am a goal-oriented and determined person*, I thought. I kept the conversation with Wladmir in mind, and a few days after I came back to the United States, I started watching Vieira's YouTube videos. I loved them! His ideas resonated with me. I liked that he was realistic, gave concrete strategies of how to make changes in life, and showed testimonies of people whose lives changed completely as a result of experiencing those strategies.

"28 Videos for an Extraordinary Life"

Vieira's work is grounded in research and his experiences as a life coach. One of his free online sets of videos is called "28 videos for an extraordinary life." I was intrigued by this set of videos—designed as a type of program—because it was created to be completed in twenty-eight days, which I thought was a very short time for people to achieve an extraordinary life.

I had heard of and even followed exercise programs, such as *P90X* and *21-Day Fix*. Those types of exercise programs promised good results if they were faithfully adhered to for a short period of time. It wasn't a surprise to see that the exercise programs worked for me, because it was just a matter of committing to the schedule and doing exactly what was asked of me. Whenever I commit to something, I follow through. Besides, I love being faithful to routines, making to-do lists, and checking items off those lists. Sometimes I think that I actually get things done just to be able to check them off the list, not really because they are important or necessary. So since I am a determined person and had successfully experienced programs that are based on a set number of days, I wondered if the "28 videos for an extraordinary life" program would work similarly to the exercise programs.

The "28 videos for an extraordinary life" program didn't have one specific or concrete goal. Instead, its goal was to help people achieve a successful life, which made me wonder even more if that was possible to accomplish in twenty-eight days. But that goal was perfect for me because, at the time, I didn't know what exactly I wanted to improve about myself. I just knew I wanted to improve myself as a person and be successful in my career. *Would I succeed at this program? What measure could be used to know if I succeeded? Would it be easy to follow through that program and put its strategies into practice?* As I thought of those questions, I scanned through the topics of each video.

Some of the topics that were addressed in the program were diligent work, focus, overcoming laziness, happiness, the power of words, and success. Simply by looking at the topics, I could imagine that it would be challenging to accomplish all that in twenty-eight days. But Vieira's excitement, confidence, and passion in what he said, and my friend's comments about the possible results from those videos, kept popping up in my mind. "There are several people who don't go to the workshop, just watch the YouTube videos, and say that their lives changed too. It's all about being committed to putting into practice the strategies that Paulo Vieira teaches and wanting to change something about you," I remembered Wladmir saying. Moreover, in the videos, Vieira often said, "Changes happen fast," "What are you doing to make a change in your life?" and "Those who act have power."[2] All of that also motivated me to consider the "28 videos for an extraordinary life" program.

---

2. Vieira, "Tem poder quem age!" (Those Who Act Have Power!).

Although I wasn't sure exactly what I wanted to improve about myself, I decided to give that set of videos a try. If I wanted to try something new, that was the right time. It was the beginning of summer, and I already knew that the fall semester was going to be very busy. In the fall, I was going to take three classes, including statistics (about which I didn't know much at all), teach two undergraduate classes, and tutor several Japanese students.

I started the "28 videos for an extraordinary life" program right away. The original program was designed to be completed in twenty-eight days so that each topic and its strategies could be focused, implemented, and practiced for at least one whole day. However, I was too intrigued and curious about the results of the program to spend an entire day on a topic. So I decided to watch more than one video every day. It wasn't enough time for me to master the strategies for the particular topic, but I took notes and kept revisiting them.

Strategies for an Extraordinary Life

Vieira presented several strategies that can lead people to a successful life.[3] Some of the strategies were taking self-responsibility, applying the 90/10 principle, focusing on existence as opposed to moments, using the social-contagion theory, implementing the Losada Ratio (also known as Losada Line), questioning, and eliminating toxic feelings. Next, I briefly explain and provide an example for each strategy, based on what I learned from Vieira's videos. To make it easy to refer to, in this book I call them *strategies for an extraordinary life*.

TAKING SELF-RESPONSIBILITY[4]
Everything that happens to us is a result of our actions, including how we think, feel, and communicate. Therefore, we should *take responsibility* for our actions and change them if they are not meeting our expectations.

---

3. Vieira, "Coaching: Revisao dos conceitos" (Coaching: Review of the Concepts).
4. Ibid.

One day, on her way back to Texas, a friend of mine forgot her cell phone in the taxi she took to the airport. When she realized that she didn't have her cell phone, she immediately blamed her sister, who didn't even live in the United States. I then asked her, "Why was it your sister's fault?"

"Because my sister always insists that I call my mom whenever I travel, to let her know that I got home safe. Since my cell phone ran out of battery, I had to ask the taxi driver to charge it on my way to the airport," she replied. "If I didn't have to call my mom, I wouldn't have charged the phone, and, consequently, I wouldn't have forgotten it in the taxi. So it's my sister's fault that I didn't remember to get the phone before leaving the taxi!"

It's clear that my friend didn't take responsibility for her actions. She blamed her sister, who was not even in the same country she was. Based on the self-responsibility principle, she should have admitted that she was probably distracted and therefore forgot to take the phone with her when she got out of the taxi. In order to take self-responsibility, we should not blame others for our own mistakes; instead, we should take responsibility for what we do. Also, we should be positive in what we think, believe, and communicate.

Applying the 90/10 Principle[5]

The *90/10 principle* refers to the notion that we should use unpleasant and challenging situations we go through as learning tools to help us grow in life. Thus, 10 percent is what happens in a situation, and 90 percent is what we do as a result of that situation. For instance, I have been very pleased with the feedback received from most of my undergraduate students, who are preservice teachers. I put a lot of effort into planning the lessons and grading students' assignments, especially because I do want them to be well prepared to work with their future

---

5. Ibid.

English-language learners. Therefore, it is gratifying to have good feed-back from them.

However, there are also some comments from students that are not as positive. After reading those comments, my first reaction was to be upset because I did not agree with what they said. But since I learned about the 90/10 principle, I now interpret the evaluations received from students in a different way. Now I remind myself that people have different learning styles, so what works for some students may not work for others. Also, I have learned to view students' negative comments as constructive feedback, which can actually make me a better instructor. In other words, instead of focusing 100 percent of my energy on the fact that some students gave me negative feedback on their evaluations, I now allocate only 10 percent of my energy to that and actually apply 90 percent of my energy to achieve positive gains from that experience, which is to improve my teaching skills. So the whole idea of 90/10 is *not* to focus on what happens to us but to focus on how we can use life situations to help us grow as a person and as a professional.

Focusing on Existence as Opposed to Moments[6]

The notion of *moments versus existence* makes us aware that we should look for existence as opposed to moments in our lives. Moments are situations that usually cost us money and bring short-term happiness. For example, when I was in college, I experienced the notion of moments several times going to parties; they brought me short-term happiness. In contrast, existence, which we usually don't pay for, refers to what brings us long-term happiness and connects us to people. For example, playing with my niece and nephews and having meaningful conversations with Kent bring me long-term happiness.

It is OK to have moments in our lives, of course, but we should focus on the notion of existence. To help us focus on existence as opposed

---

6. Ibid.

to moments, we should ask ourselves, *What is really important to me in my life? What am I doing about what is really important to me? Am I looking for existence or simply moments?*

Using the Social-Contagion Theory[7]

According to researchers such as James Fowler and Nicholas Christakis, the same way that a virus or bacterium can be contagious and spread a disease, beliefs, feelings, and behaviors can also be contagious. They call it *social contagion*—that is, the way we think and behave can influence others, and the way other people (even those who are not in direct contact with us) think and behave can also influence our beliefs and behaviors. For example, pessimistic people may make their friends and even friends of their friends pessimistic. So we should use the social-contagion theory to our advantage as a strategy to inspire and help us grow in life. We can use the social-contagion theory by choosing to be around people whose beliefs and behaviors are similar to what we believe and how we want to behave. If we want to reach success in life, we should, then, be around people who are successful or trying to be successful.

Implementing the Losada Ratio[8]

The *Losada Ratio* is a principle proposed by psychologists Marcial Losada and Barbara Fredrickson. The Losada Ratio principle posits that there is a correlation between positive expressions and success. To be exact, there is a ratio of positive to negative affect of 2.9013 as separating flourishing people from languishing people. In other words, we should focus on the qualities of those with whom we interact, especially when we have a complaint or critique to make. Based on the Losada Ratio, for each negative expression (e.g., complaint or critique), we should

---

7. Vieira, "Coaching: Contagio social" (Coaching: Social Contagion).
8. Vieira, "Coaching: Validação e linha de Losada" (Coaching: Validation and Losada Line).

have at least three positive verbal or nonverbal expressions with others. Positive verbal expressions can be a compliment on someone's appearance and actions, whereas positive nonverbal expressions can be a smile or a hug. The Losada Ratio principle is true for any type of relationship: parents-children, teacher-students, husband-wife, boss-employee, etc. As a result of a higher rate of positive connections with others, we create positive emotions within ourselves and people with whom we interact. Those positive emotions, then, benefit different areas of our lives, such as health, work performance, confidence, and relationships.

I have experienced the benefits of implementing the Losada Ratio in my relationship with Kent. It worked even without providing him with any direct verbal or nonverbal expressions. For example, one day I was having a hard time focusing on all the good qualities in Kent. It might have been because I had let little things bother me, such as noticing he had misplaced some things around the house. He's usually pretty good about putting things away—but not on that particular day, which was probably because he had rushed to get to work. Knowing that those small things shouldn't bother me, I decided to say to myself a good thing about Kent every time I saw something misplaced in the house. So as soon as I saw a cup in the bathroom, for example, I said to myself, "Kent's very thoughtful. Yesterday, he surprised me with a chai tea latte, one of my favorite drinks." After reminding myself of some of his great qualities, my mind focused on only positive thoughts about Kent. When I saw him later that day, I greeted him with a kiss and had even forgotten what had annoyed me earlier. A high rate of positive expressions definitely creates positive emotions within us.

QUESTIONING[9]

The *questioning* strategy is based on Socratic questioning. Questioning encourages us to find solutions and explore complex ideas by asking

9. Vieira, *O Poder da Acao* (The Power of Action), 209.

questions about our problems, uncertainties, and challenges. Instead of complaining, we should ask questions about issues and obstacles we might have in life. For example, when I realized I wasn't fully happy as a schoolteacher because my position at the time seemed to be limiting my potential to grow professionally, I asked myself several questions. My own questions helped me figure out what I could do to feel fully happy in my profession. I asked, "If I want to grow professionally, what do I have to do? Should I pursue my PhD degree so that I can teach in higher education? If so, where? When? If I do want to go back to graduate school, how will I pay for it? Will I quit my job to be a full-time student?" I didn't have the answers to those questions at the time. But first, we should simply come up with questions about problems, uncertainties, and obstacles we may have in the way to reach our goals. Next, we should put the questions away and revisit them only a few days later. Our minds will then be fresh and open to uncover answers to overcome obstacles and help us reach our goals.

ELIMINATING TOXIC FEELINGS[10]

Though it is not easy to do, *toxic feelings*, such as envy, anger, and ungratefulness, should be avoided. To eliminate them, we should replace envy with admiration, anger with forgiveness, and ungratefulness with gratitude. So instead of envying other people for what they have, we should admire what they have, try to learn from them, and believe we can achieve similar things. Instead of being angry at others, we should forgive them, because anger can destroy us and ruin relationships with other people around us. Instead of being ungrateful, we should frequently show our appreciation for what others do for us, because gratitude brings us positive feelings. One way to eliminate toxic feelings is by creating a positive vision of our future.

---

10. Vieira, "Coaching: Revisao dos conceitos" (Coaching: Review of the Concepts).

A Note on Applying Strategies for an Extraordinary Life
Before moving on, I want to acknowledge that it can be very challenging to apply the strategies presented above—taking self-responsibility, applying the 90/10 principle, focusing on existence as opposed to moments, using the social-contagion theory, implementing the Losada Ratio, questioning, and eliminating toxic feelings. It was definitely not easy for me to apply them in my life, but, with much persistence, I was able to incorporate them into my routine.

A Positive Vision of the Future

In Vieira's YouTube video called "How to establish a positive vision of the future," he invites us to think about an extraordinary vision of our future and create a representation of it on a poster. This vision of the future should include (a) what we look like in terms of our bodies, (b) where we see ourselves working, (c) how we see ourselves acting, (d) who we see ourselves with, and (e) where we see ourselves living.

Apart from being with Kent and becoming a professor, I had never really put too much effort into creating a vision of my future. But since I was committed to the strategies presented to me, I took some time to create a poster with my vision for the future. The vision strategy required that I create a representation of my vision on a poster with pictures and sentences written in the present tense. As I thought about what to include, I decided on the following sentences: "I am thin and fit"; "I am confident and assertive"; "I am a researcher, consultant, and professor at an American university"; "I publish journal articles and give conference presentations"; "I am focused on my goals"; "I have a new car"; and "I am happy with Kent." Each sentence was represented by a picture, to make it easier for me to visualize what I expected from myself in the future. I also wrote down deadlines next to some sentences and pictures. For example,

I wrote 2018 next to the sentence that said "I am a professor at an American university" because I plan to graduate and find a teaching job in 2018.

After completing my future-vision poster, I placed it where it could easily be seen, right in front of my office desk to remind myself of my own commitments. To reinforce those commitments, I took a picture of the poster and made it my phone's background picture. So every time I used my phone, I was reminded of my future.

Circle of Life

Vieira also devoted a video ("Prosperity of life") to discuss ten different components that shape our lives. The components are *health, social, relationship with a significant other, family, spiritual, emotional, professional, financial, intellectual,* and *service.* In the video, he kept asking, "What are you doing to address the components of life?" He also encouraged the audience to rate each component from zero to ten, zero being the lowest-rating score and ten the highest.

My ratings were very low, except for *health* and *professional.* That simple exercise made me realize that those components were unbalanced in my life. I was only prioritizing the *health* and *professional* ones. At the time, I exercised every day, ate healthily (which I still do), and spent most of the time focused on the professional aspects of life: doing schoolwork, reading and writing articles and papers, preparing classes, and grading students' assignments. Although some of these tasks may overlap with the *intellectual* component, I included all of them in the professional dimension of life because they all had to do with my current profession: a PhD student and teaching assistant.

My life-component ratings told me that I had to do something to address them somehow. *But what can I do to make sure I address them in my everyday life?* I wondered. Knowing that I love checklists,

I decided to create small goals for each component, in order to make them more concrete and to make sure each component was covered every day.

The circle-of-life component goals were created based on personal aspects that I wanted to improve, incorporate, or simply remind myself to do daily. In other words, my plan was to turn the circle-of-life goals into habits. This way, I would make sure to address all ten components in my life. Below are the goals I created for each circle-of-life component.

My Circle-of-Life Goals

- *Health*—Exercise; eat healthily.
- *Social*—Send a text message; go out with friends.
- *Family*—Send a text message; call a family member.
- *Relationship with my significant other*—Compliment; spend quality time; have a conversation with Kent.
- *Spiritual*—Say a prayer in the morning and in the evening.
- *Emotional*—Have a fifteen-minute break.
- *Professional*—Read and write academic texts; prepare classes; grade assignments.
- *Financial*—Track my expenses.
- *Intellectual*—Read books unrelated to graduate school; watch the news.
- *Service*—Help someone.

In short, the circle-of-life goals were basically created to remind myself that I should not focus my life only on the *health* and *professional* life components. Instead, I should be aware that there are other important life components that should be addressed and never ignored. Every night, I reflected on each component, putting a check mark next to the ones I addressed that day. For the components with more than one goal, I didn't have to accomplish all the goals, but at least one of them. Eventually, the circle-of-life goals became habits, helping me address each life component every day.

Neuroscientific Explanation

Since I was watching more than one video a day, I soon finished watching all "28 videos for an extraordinary life" and started watching the other YouTube videos by Vieira that were available. One day, I came across a video called "Neuroscientific explanation," an interview with a professor and neuroscientist, Tauily Taunay. That video was a turning point for me.

The interview was about why people's behavior changed after attending Vieira's workshops on emotional intelligence. Taunay said that the successful changes experienced by the workshop attendees were a result of their commitment to new sets of habits and thoughts. He explained that because of the focus on the new strategies presented at the workshops, the attendees changed the way they interpreted life situations. This new perspective in life created new feelings, which led to new behavior that ended up becoming habits. By putting into practice new behavior (in this case, the strategies learned in the workshops), the workshop attendees were changing the way their minds worked, which could be explained by neuroplasticity. According to Taunay, our beliefs are a reflection of how our neurosynapses are programmed, and the path that our neurons follow is based on how we interpret situations in our lives. Therefore, as we change our beliefs and the way we view situations, we change the path that our neurons follow and how they work. For example, by having a more positive view on different life situations, our minds will automatically start looking for more positive images.

Until then, I didn't know about the idea of neuroplasticity. I was astonished and at the time still suspicious about its positive effects on people's lives. I watched the interview over and over and even searched the term *neuroplasticity* online to find out more about it (a skill I learned in grad school—always do a fact check and look up more information about something new). In the end, I was happy to conclude that I could make my neurons work the way I wanted them to work. To me, the idea of neuroplasticity meant that since the new strategies or habits were going to become automatic in my life, the changes they would bring would eventually be instilled in me. It sounded simple, but if it were simple, why didn't so many people improve their behavior? Did people know about neuroplasticity? Why didn't I know about the power of neuroplasticity before? I had a million questions. I probably confused my neurons that day, big time!

I was eager to see changes in my life after those couple of weeks following the "28 videos for an extraordinary life" program, but it was too soon for changes to occur, especially because I wasn't allowing myself to have at least a whole day to focus on one strategy at a time. However, I kept remembering my friend Wladmir saying that I just had to be committed to the strategies shared by Vieira, put them into practice, and the results would come naturally.

By the end of the summer, I finished watching the "28 videos for an extraordinary life" and other related videos by Vieira, but I wanted to learn more about how to change my life for better. I didn't want to randomly pick a YouTube video on emotional intelligence. "What videos am I going to watch next?" I asked myself.

The Happiness Advantage

My plan was to watch videos that could build on the content I learned from Vieira. I then remembered that he mentioned that Shawn Achor said that happiness comes before success, when so many people believe that it comes after success.[11] To learn more about what Achor meant by that, I went on YouTube and searched for his name.

In the TED Talk (a nonprofit devoted to spreading ideas through short presentations) "The Happy Secret to Better Work," Achor stated that "happiness actually fuels success. Not the other way around." We tend to think that the external world mostly predicts our happiness, but actually the external world cannot predict more than 10 percent of our long-term happiness. That means that 90 percent of our long-term happiness comes from how our brains interpret the world. Achor stated that if we change the way we view the world, we can change the formula for happiness and success. That is, instead of thinking that success will take us to happiness, happiness will actually take us to success.

Moreover, according to Achor, different from what many people believe, IQ only predicts 25 percent of job successes. Social networks, optimism levels, and ability to view stress as a challenge instead of a threat predict 75 percent of job successes.[12] In other words, we tend to believe that if we work harder, we will be more successful and, consequently, feel happier. However, such belief is, simply put, *not true*. That's because if we think that we need to achieve success in order to be happy, our brains will focus on the workload, stress, and other negative aspects, which will interfere with our productivity. In reality, we should reverse that formula or way of thinking. That is, if we are happy, we will be more successful. This means that by allowing our brains to

---

11. Achor, *The Happiness Advantage*.
12. Achor, "The Happy Secret to Better Work."

experience the positive, they will perform significantly better than at negative, neutral, or stressed state, Achor explained.[13]

The advantage our brains and minds can provide is what Achor called "the happiness advantage."[14] He explained that our success rate increases when our brains are functioning in a positive state. Because a positive mind increases intelligence, energy, and creativity, this increase makes the brain work 31 percent better. Furthermore, he said, we can maximize our brains' potential by not only believing that happiness leads to success, but also by acting in a way to make happiness lead us to success. According to Achor, as a result of this mind-set, we become happy *now* as opposed to waiting to be happy *later* (only after we achieve success). But how could I make my mind more positive? I kept asking myself that question as I watched his lecture. The answer is to create a workout for my brain.

Brain Exercises

As Achor highlighted, many people tend to think that the formula for happiness is to first reach success. However, people should *be happy first*, and then they will reach success. We can follow that formula (happiness → success) by creating a positive mind-set.[15] As I learned more about the brain, it became clear to me that just like we need to exercise our bodies if we want to have a fit and healthy body, we also need to exercise our brains if we want to have a positive mind.

In his TED Talk, Achor provided five concrete research-based exercises for lasting positive change: to (1) show gratitude, (2) journal positive experiences, (3) engage in physical exercise, (4) meditate, and (5) perform random acts of kindness.[16]

---

13. Ibid.
14. Ibid.
15. Ibid.
16. Ibid.

The first exercise comprised *writing down or sharing with someone three things for which we are grateful.* The three things don't have to be big or special. We could simply be grateful for having had a favorite sandwich for lunch, for example. What is important is to show gratitude. The second exercise consisted of *journaling one positive experience* that we had in the previous twenty-four hours. By writing about a pleasant experience, we relive that experience and, as a result, we feel the same good feelings we had while it happened. This type of recall improves our mood. The third exercise was *engaging in physical exercise* for at least thirty minutes, three times a week. Physical exercise promotes the delivery of oxygen to the brain, so it helps us think more clearly and more efficiently. Physical exercise also helps improve our metabolism and raise our endorphin (feel-good hormone) levels. The fourth exercise was to *meditate* for at least two minutes. Meditation has multiple benefits, not the least of which is how it calms our minds and helps us focus, thus counteracting the constant multitasking behavior today's world imposes on us. Finally, the last exercise was to *perform random acts of kindness*, which could entail helping someone through a difficult situation or simply writing an e-mail or text message praising someone. By performing acts of kindness, we make someone feel good and contribute to making the world a better place. Moreover, when we do good things, we also feel good in return. Achor suggested that these exercises be done for at least twenty-one days in a row, in order to turn them into habits and train our minds to think positively.[17]

After pondering the benefits of the brain exercises, I realized they would not only bring more positivity into my life in general but also help me succeed in my academic life and keep me healthier. It was still the end of summer, but I was already feeling overwhelmed with a paper, a conference proposal, and a systematic literature review that needed to be finished before the fall semester. So I knew that once the semester

---

17. Ibid.

started, I would only feel more overwhelmed with all my graduate-school texts to read, papers to write, classes to teach, and assignments to grade. Since I wouldn't be able to add one extra day in the week to get all my workload done and wouldn't want to feel stressed out like all the other semesters, I thought that the brain exercises would be the solution to my foreseen problem. I then decided to immediately start putting those brain exercises into practice. And I did, the very next day.

WHAT ABOUT YOU?

- *Do you take responsibility for your own actions?*
- *Think of an unpleasant situation that has happened to you. How could you have applied the 90/10 principle in that situation?*
- *What is really important to you in your life? What are you doing about what is really important to you? Are you looking for existence or simply moments in life?*
- *Knowing that we should use the social-contagion theory to our advantage as a strategy to help us grow in life, who would you like to be around? Who would you like to "contaminate" you?*
- *How would the Losada Ratio strategy improve your life?*
- *Think of a problem or challenge you have at the moment. What questions come to your mind as you try to find a possible solution for it?*
- *What toxic feelings should you eliminate? How can you eliminate them?*
- *What would your vision poster look like?*
- *What are you doing to address the components of the circle of life? Which concrete goals would you create for each component?*
- *What are three things you are grateful for?*

- *Is physical exercise part of your routine? If not, how can you incorporate physical exercise into your routine?*
- *Describe a positive experience you had in the last twenty-four hours.*
- *What is one act of kindness that you can do tomorrow?*

Two

REFLECTING ON MY NEW-ME JOURNEY

Simply putting into practice actions to improve something about ourselves is not enough. It is also important to reflect on the implementation of those actions to find out if they are working or not. A good way to reflect on our personal growth process is comparing what we were like *before* we started taking actions to improve something about ourselves to *after* we started taking such actions. This comparison can indicate if our behaviors and attitudes are leading us in the direction we want to go. Having said that, in this chapter I reflect on my journey, using anecdotes, by comparing *before* my new-me journey to *after* my new-me journey.

As part of my new-me-journey process, every day for a month, I went through the checklist of goals for each component of the circle of life, did physical exercise, performed an act of kindness, wrote about a good experience, and made a list of three things for which I was grateful. I also took notes of small victories I had as a result of my commitment to the circle-of-life goals and brain exercises. I confess that I didn't do any meditation. I tried to meditate, but my mind would not stop spinning for even two minutes. So I gave it up, which made me feel disappointed with myself. About a month later, I decided to reflect on my journey. Until then, I hadn't shared my journey with Kent or anyone else, except with my therapist at the time; I will call her Dr. Sarah. Knowing myself, if I told someone about my new-me journey, I would certainly follow through this personal commitment. So I decided to share with Dr. Sarah my reflection on my new-me journey.

Before My New-Me Journey

I reminded Dr. Sarah of how I was before my new-me journey so that I could compare it with how I was after starting the journey. I told her that before my new-me journey, I was pessimistic and moody, didn't smile much, lacked self-esteem, and feared talking to people who intimidated me. Maybe those negative characteristics I had were the ones that unconsciously led me to the urgency to improve myself as a person through my new-me journey.

I didn't have to elaborate much on those characteristics about me to Dr. Sarah because she was already aware of them. But allow me to elaborate on at least a few of them, so you have a better idea of what I was like before diving into my new-me journey.

MOODY

I used to be very moody. Little things that went wrong or happened in a way that I didn't expect would often change my mood. As a result, my bad mood would negatively affect my relationship with Kent and whoever was around me. For example, I remember one evening that was supposed to be fun and turned out to be annoying.

Kent and I were getting ready to go out to celebrate a friend's birthday. We told our friend to meet us at our place so we would only need to take one car. He arrived at the exact time we planned, but Kent and I were not ready to leave yet. I was closer to being ready than Kent; I just had to finish putting on some makeup. Noticing that I was almost ready and not giving much importance to my makeup (I guess), Kent asked me to do some little chores in the house, such as turn on the outside lights and turn off the TV. Well, by the time I finished doing the chores he had asked me to and putting on my makeup, he was already ready to leave.

Our friend didn't seem to mind waiting for us. However, since Kent doesn't like to make people wait, he was annoyed when I was still not ready by the time he was ready. Of course I wasn't! I would have been ready, standing by the door like he was, if he hadn't asked me to do those chores. Annoyed, Kent said to our friend, "Sorry for having to wait. But you know Angelica. She is never ready on time." I couldn't believe what I was hearing! I should have said something to show that I didn't agree with what he was saying, but I didn't bother saying anything, sure that he would not accept my arguments and because the back-and-forth would not take us anywhere. Result: I was in a bad mood for the rest of the evening. The only good thing was that soon the day was going to be over, and a new day would begin. Knowing myself, when I got in a bad mood, it would last the rest of the day.

LACK OF ASSERTIVENESS AND CONFIDENCE

Besides being moody, I used to lack assertiveness and confidence. I grew up being told to say *yes* to everyone because I was expected to please others. So I did. I followed that "rule" very well, such as one time when I went to the bank in Brazil to collect an unemployment check. After talking to the manager, I left the bank having one more bank account and joining an investment program, but without my unemployment check. Yes, it was that bad! As long as it wasn't going to physically hurt me, I would say *yes* to everybody who asked me for help or offered me something.

My lack of assertiveness was supported by my insecurity and shyness, which often made me feel uncomfortable talking to acquaintances, strangers, or people I didn't know well. Because of that, I would avoid running into people I was not close to, such as classmates or professors, so that I would not have to talk to them uncomfortably. I would imagine running out of things to say and having that awkward moment of silence in the conversation when both people don't know what to say or do.

I often felt this uneasy feeling while living in the graduate dorm at the University of Massachusetts Amherst. At the dorm, all the women from my floor had to share two big restrooms, so it was common to run into acquaintances in there. Since I felt uncomfortable when that happened, I decided to not use the restroom during "rush hour," around eight thirty every morning, when many people were getting ready. I was lucky that my school schedule allowed me to do that. My idea was successful. I started to see people in the restroom less often, until one day when I ran into a woman who lived next to my room. Surprised to see me, she said, "Where have you been? I don't see you anymore." If only she knew how hard I was trying not to see her or others.

Kent is part of another example that comes to my mind to show how hard I avoided feeling uncomfortable while talking to people who were not close to me. Before we had started dating, Kent and I took a course together in the spring of 2005. Besides being a PhD student, Kent was also a research assistant at the time, which meant that he spent most of the day on campus. During that semester, I didn't mind running into him because we had the course content and assignments to talk about. However, in the following semester, after seeing him in the School of Education hallway, I would do my best to avoid running into him again. That's because when we saw each other, he gave me a free pass and invited me to go to the dance studio that he ran on Wednesday evenings in a town next to Amherst. At the time, I should have said something like, "Thanks for the pass, but I'm not sure if I will be able to go," or, "It's so nice of you to give me a free pass! I will try to go there someday." However, embarrassed to refuse his invitation, I actually said, "Thanks! I will definitely go there." But I knew I would not. I didn't have anyone to go with me. I didn't know how to get there. I didn't want to take the bus at night, especially because it was very cold. Besides, I didn't even like dancing.

"Why did I say that I was going?" I asked myself. "Now I hope I don't run into him, because I am sure he is going to ask why I didn't go to his dance."

Sure enough, in the following week, right after my afternoon class, he saw me at the front door with my classmate and friend Silvia as we waited for her husband to pick us up. I usually walked to the dorm, but I never refused a ride back to the dorm, especially on very cold days.

"Hi, Angelica!" Kent greeted me.

"Oh, hi," I said without much excitement in seeing him.

"The dance was great last week. You should have come," he said.

"Sorry, I couldn't go." I should have stopped there, but I didn't. What did I say next? "But I will go to the dance next week." No, I would not. Why did I say that?

Then he said, "Great! See you there, then. Don't forget you have the free pass."

"I won't," I said and then immediately thought, *Oh my goodness! Now I really have to hide from this man. I know I am not going to his dance, and I won't know what to say if he brings it up again.*

The following week, about five minutes before my afternoon class was over, I asked my classmate Silvia—who knew nothing about Kent, by the way—to text her husband to ask him to pick us up. We already knew that he was going to pick us up, but Silvia usually asked him to leave the house after the class was over. That meant we had to wait a few minutes for him, which I was trying to avoid so I didn't run the risk of seeing Kent. I used the cold weather as an excuse to have Silvia text her husband.

"You know, it's very cold today. So maybe you should text your husband now so he is here by the time our class is over. This way we won't have to wait for him in this cold weather," I told her.

I guess she didn't realize my excuse didn't even make sense. Yes, it was cold, but we were going to wait for him indoors, so it didn't really matter how long we waited. But I was happy to see that she texted him. Unfortunately, my plan didn't work. I ended up having to wait for Silvia's husband for a few minutes. And guess who showed up? Kent.

As soon as I saw Kent at the end of the hallway coming toward the building entrance, where I was, I turned my body to the other side, hoping that he wouldn't recognize my back. My plan didn't work again. He came right around me and said, "Hi, Angelica!"

Oh no! I immediately thought. "Hi," I said.

"How are you?" he asked.

"I'm fine. And you?"

"I'm fine." He went on to say, "It's too bad that you didn't come to the dance. It was fun!"

"I'm sorry. But…"

Don't say it. Don't say it, I thought.

"But I will go next week," I continued. *Oh no! I said it again!* I couldn't believe that it was so hard for me to simply say *no*.

The same dialogue ended up happening three or four times that semester. Only later, when we started dating, Kent told me that he was "stalking" me, which reminded me of the *Seinfeld* episode called "The Stakeout." No wonder I would always "run into" him every week at the same place and time during that semester. In case you're curious, here's what happened next. The following semester, after coming back from Brazil, I decided to make more friends in the United States. So I thought that going to a dance would be a good place for that. I then e-mailed Kent to ask if I could still use the free pass he had given to me. He said yes, so I convinced a friend to go with me to the dance. A few days after going to the dance, I went on dates with Kent; the more I got to know him, the more I liked him.

My lack of assertiveness didn't help my insecurity at all. A thousand questions would very frequently come to my mind just to doubt myself. I would ask myself, "*Who am I* to say that?"; "*Who am I* to do that?"; "Angelica, listen to your accent; who's going to believe *you* with that accent and face of a foreigner?"; or "Angelica, *you* have such a young face; people won't take you seriously. So don't even bother talking to them."

I do look much younger than my age. I know a lot of people would love to have a younger look. Eventually, I will too, but not now. Many times it bothers me that I am mistaken for someone much younger. Several times while working as a middle-school teacher, I was mistaken for a student! Mind you, at that particular school, students were between ten and thirteen years old, and I was in my midthirties!

My lack of assertiveness was also present in how I handled disagreements. In order to please others, from a very young age, I not only learned that it was proper to say *yes* but also to avoid arguing. As a result, even in my late thirties, I would still walk away, be silent, or simply not counterargue when someone argued with me. For example, when I was working at a middle school, a teacher came into my classroom during an in-service day. Pointing to two computer desks that belonged to the ESL classroom (the classroom I used), the teacher said in a very demanding tone, "Those computer desks belong to my classroom."

Surprised, I said in an unsure tone, "To your classroom? I thought they were bought for the ESL students to use." The truth was that I didn't *think* they were bought for the ESL students—I was *absolutely* sure those desks were bought for the ESL classroom because that was what the school principal had explicitly told me before she purchased them. So why did I say *I thought*? To avoid arguing with her, of course. My nonconfrontational attitude cost me those two computer desks.

Disagreeing with me, the teacher said, "No, these computer desks were bought for the classroom that I use."

I simply said, "OK. You can take them. But where am I going to put the computers?"

"On the table that I had my student computers on," she said.

So with my help, she replaced the computer desks from the ESL classroom with the table from her classroom. As we moved the furniture, the bilingual teacher, whose classroom was right next to mine, looked confused. Then she asked me, "Angelica, aren't those computer desks for your students?"

"Yes, that's what I thought," I said. Again, I said, *I thought*.

"I'm sure they were for your students!" the bilingual teacher said. "I heard when the principal told you she was going to buy them for the ESL classroom because your students are required to use a computer program every day. You shouldn't have let her take your classroom computer desks."

I finally confessed, "I know. I just wanted to avoid a conflict."

Here's one more example that illustrates my lack of assertiveness, which this time led me to sleep on the floor. As I mentioned earlier, I am a PhD student at Texas A&M University in College Station, a city two hours away from Houston. To avoid commuting several days every week, I decided to spend two nights a week in College Station. A friend allowed me to stay in her apartment during those nights. I spent the whole day on campus and just went to the apartment to sleep on an air mattress that she lent me. The sleeping arrangement was completely fine until her father came to visit her for a few weeks.

Before he arrived, I asked her, "Where is he going to sleep?"

"On the air mattress," she replied.

But *I* slept on the air mattress. So I asked, "Do you have another air mattress?"

"No," she said.

"I'm asking this because I can bring an air mattress from my house," I explained.

"It's not necessary because I want to buy another air mattress anyway," she told me.

"OK," I said.

Well, it wasn't really what she did.

Later that month, close to ten o'clock, when I got to her apartment to spend the night, her father was there, and I saw only one air mattress. Thinking that the new one was still in a box somewhere, I asked, "Where's the new air mattress that you bought?"

"What new air mattress?" she asked, looking puzzled.

"The one you said you were going to buy."

"I said I was going to buy a new air mattress?" she said in a surprised tone.

"Yes, you did. I offered to bring my air mattress from Houston, but you said it wasn't necessary because you were going to buy a new one anyway."

She simply said, "Oh, I said that? Sorry. I didn't buy it."

Trying to solve the problem, I asked, "Can your father sleep on your bed since you have a double bed?" She looked at me with a face that said "No way!" Curious about the sleeping arrangements, I asked, "So where am I going to sleep?"

"I don't know," she replied.

Exhausted and sleepy, I just said, "It's fine. I'll sleep on the floor."

"OK."

I couldn't believe I had given that solution to the problem! I should have suggested something else. Of course I didn't want her father to sleep on the floor, but I should have been assertive and requested a better solution from her, especially because she was the one who caused the problem. We wouldn't have gone through that situation if she hadn't told me I didn't have to bring my air mattress. By the way, she wasn't sharing her apartment with me for free. I was paying $350 a month to spend only two nights a week there. And in that particular month, I only spent three nights, including the one I slept on the floor. Again, there I was not speaking up for myself and avoiding confrontations. Up to what point was it healthy to act like that? Yes, I was avoiding confrontations, but I was also piling up hurt feelings inside of me. How healthy was it to internalize these feelings?

FINAL THOUGHTS ON "BEFORE MY NEW-ME JOURNEY"
I have gone through many other similar situations where I didn't speak up for myself. But now, reflecting back on those moments, I realize that I didn't only say yes or purposely avoided confrontations simply to please others. I also acted that way because I didn't have much self-esteem and felt inferior to and intimidated by some people. As a result, many times I felt that there were occasions when people took advantage of my willingness to help, my low self-esteem, and my lack of assertiveness. However, my new-me journey was starting to show positive results, including in terms of assertiveness.

After My New-Me Journey

In my sessions with Dr. Sarah, I began sharing how I was doing about a month after my new-me journey had started. Looking back at my victory notes taken during the month when I put into practice the strategies for an extraordinary life, circle-of-life component goals, and brain exercises (described in chapter 1), it was clear that I had improved as a person. Compared to before my new-me journey, I was more positive, I was able to control my mood, and I showed that I could act assertively and confidently.

POSITIVE

I was a more positive person through my actions and thoughts. For example, instead of nagging Kent about what he needed to get done in the house, I was complimenting him more often. I was also trying to bring positivity into all my conversations. For instance, throughout the fall semester, I ended the weekly meetings with two people from the Undergraduate Peer Mentor program who helped me with my undergraduate students, by having each of us share "good stuff" that had happened to us that week. When tutoring my Japanese students, I started the sessions by asking, "Tell me something good that happened today." At the end of my weekly calls to my aunt and uncle, I also encouraged them to share something good that had happened to them lately.

Moreover, I was being more positive by avoiding judging people— something that I used to do in the past. I kept myself away from gossip because if I judged someone, I would immediately feel bad and regret my negative comments. I was proud of myself one day when I had many opportunities to judge others while talking to some friends. But already knowing how I was going to feel as a result of saying negative things about others, I controlled myself, and if I didn't have anything good to say, I didn't say anything at all. In the end, I felt proud of myself and happy for not judging others.

I noticed that not only was I becoming a positive person, but I was also easily noticing negative comments from others. Even after years of friendship with some relatives and friends, only then I realized how negative some of them were. For example, I instantly noticed negativity from a friend, who is a professor, when we were talking one day.

"It seems that you and your husband do everything together. Commute together. Cook together. Work together. Go to a coffee shop together. Travel everywhere together. You two seem to be very good friends!" I said to her. She had never mentioned having any friends besides her husband. So I asked her, "Do you have other friends besides him where you live?"

"No. I wish I had friends there, but it's hard for me to make friends because I spend most of the time working. So I would have to make friends at work," she replied.

"Why don't you make friends at work? Aren't your colleagues nice?"

"Yes, they are. But I can't be friends with them," she said.

"Why not?" I insisted.

"Because if I become friends with them, I would share personal plans and, as a result, they would hurt me by telling other colleagues, including my supervisor, about my plans," she explained.

I was very confused by what she was saying. Why would people hurt their own friends? If they wanted to hurt their friends, they wouldn't be called friends. To better understand what she meant, I asked, "What do you think your potential friends would do to you?"

"Well, here's an example. In order to be promoted at work, I need to publish a book and several academic articles. If I become friends with someone from work, I would probably share my plans of getting pregnant in the near future," she said.

"OK. I don't see any problems with that. Any good friends would share that with each other," I commented.

"The problem is that I wouldn't want some colleagues to know about my plans to get pregnant, because they would probably think I wasn't going to be a productive professor since my focus could be on having a baby," she said.

"But how would those colleagues know about your plans?" I asked, still confused.

"My hypothetical friends would most likely tell them," she explained.

"But you don't know that they would do that," I kept insisting.

"But they might," she said.

I gave up. I couldn't believe how negative she was letting herself be to justify why it wasn't her fault that she couldn't have any friends at work. It was so much easier to be positive by simply saying, "That's right. I should try to make new friends at work. They seem to be nice people. I just have to make sure to trust them before I share something personal." Instead, her choice was to be negative, which required more arguments and creativity.

In addition to the conversation with this friend, I have several examples of short dialogues with relatives and friends who brought up something negative in the first few minutes of conversation. "I had a good week, but you know…" "I am fine, but…" "Yes, I got that done, but…" and so on. To my surprise, all that negativity was starting to bother me, especially when my relatives and friends would refuse to see the positive side that was available to them.

STABLE MOOD

Although I wasn't specifically trying to improve my mood, I did notice my mood was becoming more stable than before. It must have been a result of the positive mind-set that my new habits had created. Writing down three gratitudes and doing an act of kindness every day were definitely making my mind look for positivity in my life.

I remember one day saying to Dr. Sarah, "I haven't told Kent about my new-me journey. So I wonder if he will notice any changes in me as a result of it."

She replied, "Well, I think he will start seeing changes in you. But if he doesn't seem to notice anything after six months, you should tell him about your journey."

Dr. Sarah was right. Kent did start noticing some changes in me, such as my good mood. One day, as we were getting in the car, he said, "You *are* in a good mood today! What happened?"

"Nothing special. I'm simply in a good mood," I said. I wasn't surprised by his *What happened?* question. I think that he was so used to my usual roller-coaster mood that it was strange to see me in a good mood for a long period of time. Kent's question made me realize that finally I didn't need anything special to happen in my life to be in a good mood. I didn't need to buy or accomplish anything. I just needed to continue practicing the strategies (e.g., performing an act of kindness and writing down gratitudes) that I had learned to keep a positive mind-set.

I realized that my positive mind-set was really working when I caught myself smiling even at moments when I didn't expect to smile. That happened, for example, when Kent complained about something I did or didn't do. Instead of being passive and letting my facial expression show I didn't agree with his point of view (like before my new-me journey), there I was not only with a big smile but also assertively stating my point of view to him. Unconsciously, I was also acting the same way toward other people. Instead of getting upset and showing my upset feelings through facial expressions or attitudes, I would simply smile and speak up for myself.

The act of smiling was definitely helping me keep my good mood and avoid getting upset. Months later, Tal Ben-Shahar, author of books in the field of positive psychology, assured me that I was doing the right thing by reacting with a smile and assertiveness as opposed to signs of anger. In his book *Choose the Life You Want*, he said, "Modify your usual reaction even slightly and you might find that you're piloting yourself and those around you on a different course—a much more pleasant journey."[18] That was exactly what was happening to me: my smile was leading me to a more pleasant journey.

ASSERTIVE AND CONFIDENT

I told Dr. Sarah that I was able to be assertive and confident. I was finally able to say no and speak up for myself when necessary. Besides applying

---

18. Ben-Shahar, *Choose the Life You Want*, Choice 38.

the strategies for an extraordinary life and brain exercises, I also looked for role models, starting with Kent. He is a very assertive and confident man, from whom I can learn a lot. So I started observing him to learn what I could do to become assertive. I also observed friends, news anchors, and TV characters, especially women about my age. I noticed that I didn't have to be rude to be assertive. I noticed that being assertive wasn't a bad trait. On the contrary, it showed a strong and confident personality. It was unfortunate that I wasn't taught to be assertive when I was younger. But it wasn't too late. I could learn how to be assertive now. I had tried it before but had no success—probably because I wasn't persistent enough in trying to improve my assertiveness. However, the strategies for an extraordinary life and brain exercises had indirectly empowered me to become more confident—and it was actually working.

Before saying *yes* or *no*, I was able to stop, consider the situation, remind myself that *no* was also an option, and only then decide if the answer should be *yes* or *no*. At the end of July, I had the chance to put these steps into practice with a friend. We first met at Burger King because her two daughters, around two and five years old, wanted something to eat. After they ate, they played in the playground as my friend and I caught up with each other's lives. From Burger King, we went to Target, where she bought some Play-Doh for her daughters. As we were leaving Target, I asked, "Where are we going now?"

She said, "To your house."

"My house?" I looked at her, surprised. "You know I have no toys for the girls to play with."

"It's OK. They will work with the Play-Doh," she said.

I used to love Play-Doh as a child, so I know that kids can, unintentionally, leave pieces of it all over the house. With that in mind, and having just cleaned the house, I immediately asked, "And who's going to pick up after they use the Play-Doh?"

Without hesitation, my friend said, "You!"

I instantly thought, *Here's my big chance to be assertive*, especially to this friend who was very assertive. She would very comfortably and politely say no whenever she didn't want something. So why couldn't *I* be assertive with her?

"Me?" I paused. "Sorry. We can't go to my house because I am not going to clean up after your daughters," I told her, nicely but firmly. "Since it's too far to go to your house, let's think of a public place where the girls can play. How about McDonald's? They have a cool playground there," I suggested.

"That's a good idea! Let's try that. Where's the closest McDonald's from here?" she asked with a smile, showing that she accepted and wasn't upset by my suggestion.

I know that saying no is easy for many people, but it was such a challenge for me. I always felt that by saying no, I was being mean. However, little by little, I was learning that it was OK to give *no* as an answer and still be polite. I just had to be assertive. And I was starting to be.

Here's another example. A few months later, I went to a store to buy a box of chocolate gel packs. The little gel packs can be bought individually or in a box of twenty-four. That day, there was only one open box. I counted the gel packs that were in it, hoping that the box was still full. "Twenty-three," I told the salesman.

"We can only sell the box if there are twenty-four gel packs," he said.

Months ago, I would have said, "That's too bad. OK. So I will buy the gel packs individually," which would be more expensive than buying the whole box. Instead, I decided to use my new assertiveness skills and asked, "Since I only need one gel pack to make it twenty-four, can I take a different-flavored gel pack to make it twenty-four?"

"No, we can't do that because it's going to mess up our inventory," he replied.

Again, months ago, I would have simply accepted what he said. However, I wanted to keep putting my new skills into practice. So I said, "I understand that. But the other day when I came here, I ran into the same situation, and the salesperson offered me a different-flavored gel pack so that I could buy the whole box." He listened to me, but he didn't say anything immediately. Out of arguments, I said, "OK. Even though there are only twenty-three gels, I will pay for the whole box because it'll still be cheaper than buying them individually."

First, he said, "OK." He agreed, even though he previously said he couldn't sell the whole box if there weren't twenty-four gels. Soon after, he added, "I'll give you a discount since the box isn't complete."

Gladly, I said, "Great! Thanks!" The discount was only about two dollars, but that wasn't the point. I was happy to get the discount because it was a result of my assertiveness. If I hadn't argued with the salesman, I wouldn't have gotten the discount, and I would have left the store thinking, *I should have said something.* It was a minor accomplishment, but I left the store feeling proud of myself.

My new assertiveness skills, which came with confidence, were making me more communicative and comfortable when engaging in conversations. I stopped avoiding people who were not close to me simply because I might not have something to say or know how to end the conversation. For example, there is a professor I really admire. However, she's very quiet, and it seems that the awkward silence in conversations doesn't bother her. But it bothered me and made me feel uncomfortable. I felt the pressure of always having something to say and being able to carry out the conversation, which, many times, is a challenge for introverts like me. So I would avoid running into her. Not anymore. One day when I was about to leave the teachers' lounge at the university, this particular professor, who was on sabbatical, came in. My immediate thought surprised me. Instead of thinking, *Oh, no, I should have come here later. What am I going to say? How am I going to end the conversation?* I actually thought, *Wow, what a nice surprise! I haven't seen her in a long time!* So that was exactly what I said.

"Hi! It's nice to see you, too. How are you?" she asked.

"I'm fine. How are you?"

"Fine."

"I'm sure you are having a very productive sabbatical semester." She's a very active researcher, which is something I admire in her. She had encouraged and invited many of her students to do research with her. Of course, I accepted the invitation. I do my best not to pass up a research opportunity.

She smiled and nodded, agreeing with me.

"I enjoyed researching and writing my part of the literature review of your research project," I told her. "But I confess it wasn't easy to find information about it."

"Yes, that's true."

"There is very little research about that topic. No wonder you chose to research it."

She smiled. Then she asked, "How's your semester going?"

"It's going well, but very busy! I'm taking three courses and teaching two classes."

She looked surprised.

"But I enjoy teaching them, and the courses I'm taking are interesting," I told her. "So I don't mind having a busy semester."

It was time to wrap up the conversation because I needed to get ready for class, so I said to her, "Well, it was great seeing you. Hope you have a productive rest of semester. Let me know what else you would like me to do for your research project."

"You, too. I will."

With that, I left. The conversation had gone very well, with no awkward silence. To my surprise, that brief exchange with her was natural.

Something similar happened other times. An example of that was when I saw an acquaintance one day at a parking lot. Instead of pretending not to see him, without hesitating, I stopped the car just to say hi to him. We ended up talking for about ten minutes. I was amazed with myself, especially because I was not even hesitating to engage in conversations with people who were just acquaintances. Moreover, I didn't feel intimidated by or inferior to others. On the contrary, I felt confident and ready to engage in any conversation, including ones that could be challenging.

WORK PERFORMANCE

I also shared with Dr. Sarah that I noticed improvement in my academic work performance. My brain was definitely working faster than before my new-me journey. I could more easily understand challenging texts and better control stress. As a result, I was more productive and confident in my work performance. I'm sure my work performance improvement was connected to the positive emotions I was experiencing through my new-me journey. In his book *The Happiness Advantage*, Achor explains:

> Positive emotions flood our brains with dopamine and serotonin, chemicals that not only make us feel good, but dial up the learning centers of our brains to higher levels. They help us organize new information, keep that information in the brain longer, and retrieve it faster later on. And they enable us to make and sustain more neural connections, which allows us to think more quickly and creatively, become more skilled at complex analysis and problem solving, and see and invent new ways of doing things.[19]

I first noticed improvement in my academic work performance at the end of the summer, when I had to submit a systematic literature review paper—a paper in which the author systematically synthesizes the

---

19. Achor, *The Happiness Advantage*, Principle #1, Your Brain on Happiness section.

findings of several articles—and a conference proposal. I had already spent about six weeks working on the systematic literature review paper on learning a second language through interactions. The paper was taking longer than I thought, so before I realized, only a couple of days were left to complete it. After following some systematic procedures to identify the articles needed for this paper, to finish my work, I had to make sure to read all thirty-two peer-reviewed articles that I had found about my topic, complete an annotated bibliography for each of them, and finally, write the paper. Thinking of everything that still needed to get done for the paper, I said to myself, "I will never be able to finish all that in time." But my thought was immediately interrupted by Achor's words. In an interview, he said he had conducted studies that showed that people get stressed out because they tend to focus on things that are out of their control. Therefore, people should be realistic, accept the fact that they are not in control of certain things, and actually focus on things in their control.[20] This way they will avoid stress and be more productive. So I decided to put those research findings into practice.

For the last two days that I had to write the paper, I made a list of what was in my control: finish reading the articles, completing the annotated bibliographies, writing the paper, allowing my mind and body to take breaks, and being committed to the schedule I had created. That said, I worked in chunks of forty-five minutes, giving myself a fifteen-minute break in between. During the short breaks, I talked to Kent, watched TV, had a snack, checked my phone for any missed calls or text messages, or even took a short nap. In the evening, I gave myself a two-hour break so that I could exercise, take a shower, and have dinner. I should also mention that working in chunks of forty-five minutes was perfect because I kept reminding myself, "Angelica, you can do it. It's only for forty-five minutes. Focus!" It seems that my mind didn't realize I was tricking it by letting it think I was going to work only for forty-five

---

20. Achor, interview.

minutes. The fact that I told myself, "Focus!" as I put my cell phone away also seemed to help my mind get rid of all possible distractions, including the thought of maybe not having time to complete that paper by the due date.

A few days later, after submitting the paper, I received feedback on it from a high-achieving doctoral candidate who worked at the time as a writer consultant. Before we began discussing what needed to be improved, deleted, revised, or added to the paper, the writer consultant said, "Before we go through the details of the paper, I want to say that I am impressed with it. There is room for improvement, but it is already well written."

"Really?" I asked doubtfully. I wasn't confident about the quality of my writing because most of the paper was written two days prior to the deadline. In addition to that, it was written in chunks of forty-five minutes with several breaks in between. It was the first time I had tried writing an academic assignment that way. Before that, driven by procrastination, I wrote for several hours in a row, without breaks, but with anxiety and stress. Even though back then I received good feedback on my writing, I would feel exhausted, with low energy, and stressed during the whole process. However, this time was different. I still received good feedback, but I didn't feel exhausted, have low energy, or feel stressed during the writing process. On the contrary, I felt energetic and motivated to write. During the writing process, I also started seeing that assignment as a meaningful task as opposed to a mandatory task that needed to get done.

The feedback I received on that particular paper showed that (a) writing in chunks, (b) allowing my mind to rest, (c) being aware of what was in my control and what was not in my control, (d) focusing all my energy, thoughts, and actions on what I could do toward the assignments, and (e) believing in myself led me to not only succeed in my writing and avoid feeling stressed about it but also made me see that assignment through positive lenses. What started as a task ended up as a paper that could be published (which, in the field of academia, is what really matters) and be informative and helpful for language teachers and researchers. Moreover, writing that paper put me ahead of the game in terms of my dissertation, because the topics of the paper and the dissertation were the same.

This experience showed me that there are times when it is better to take one step back in order to take two steps forward. Also, I learned the importance of not letting distractions, such as negative thoughts, take over my mind. Instead, I should make room for positive thoughts by reminding myself that I am capable of completing the assignments and by focusing on what I can control. In case you are wondering, the conference proposal was accepted, and now I am trying to publish the paper in an academic journal.

FINAL THOUGHTS ON "AFTER MY NEW-ME JOURNEY"

Not long after my conversation with the writer consultant, one of the notes I shared with Dr. Sarah read: *Today, I caught myself thinking, "I don't recognize myself. I've been so much more patient, positive, generous, confident, and communicative than ever!"* So I asked her if all those changes were a result of everything that I was putting into practice such as the strategies for an extraordinary life, circle-of-life component goals, positive vision of my future, and brain exercises. She said they were.

I left her office with the desire to continue with my new-me journey and learn more about what I could do to keep improving myself as a person. I still didn't know exactly what goal I wanted to reach. So far, I just knew I didn't want to be the Angelica from before my new-me journey anymore.

WHAT ABOUT YOU?

- *Have you ever taken actions to improve something about yourself? If so, what actions have you taken?*
- *What were you like before you started putting those actions into practice?*
- *What were you like after you started putting those actions into practice?*
- *Did the actions work for you? Did they help you improve what you wanted to improve about yourself?*
- *Is there anything you would like to improve about yourself? If so, what is it? What actions can you take to see that improvement in yourself? Take notes during the process of applying your actions so you can reflect on them later.*

Three

DISCOVERING HAPPINESS

Summer was now officially over, and the fall semester had started. That fall was the turning point in my new-me journey because it was when I discovered happiness in the midst of a crazy-busy semester. My first week of classes alerted me that the semester was going to be busier than I had imagined. In the fall, I was going to teach two undergraduate classes and take three courses as a doctoral student. Everybody who teaches knows that teaching is a time-consuming job. Besides the time we spend in the classroom, we also have to prepare lesson plans, create and grade assignments, answer students' e-mails, and deal with any issues related to the course that may appear throughout the semester.

As for the courses I was going to take (philosophy theories, task-based language teaching, and statistics), all three were going to be time consuming because in addition to the heavy load of reading required for each one, the professors' teaching styles and assignments showed that they had very high expectations for students.

In my philosophy course, each student was expected to become an expert on a particular philosophy theory and philosopher. Then, we had to apply that expertise in every class discussion and debate. My philosophy professor was not only a professor but a philosopher too. So you can imagine his passion and excitement for the course content as well as his high expectations for his students' learning.

My task-based language teaching course was taught by my adviser, who was constantly pushing her advisees to graduate as soon as possible. That meant she took advantage of teaching that course to have her students start working on their dissertation literature review and proposal.

As for my statistics course, it was taught by an internationally well-known and respected statistician who is a distinguished professor (a professor who has received extraordinary recognition for the scholarly attainment in his or her discipline or field) and, by the way, the author of the required course textbook. I will call him Dr. James. There were students at Texas A&M University who looked forward to taking a course with him. Others chose to take his course because they were advised to do so, which was my case. Many students hesitated taking courses with Dr. James because his classes were known to be challenging. This was so true that my own adviser (who constantly had high expectations for her advisees) said to me, "It's OK if you get a B in his course." A B grade was acceptable because many professors and students believed that a B in his course was actually an A in any other course.

Dr. James seemed to consider his students experts in statistics, or at least in learning skills. He definitely cared for our learning, but his strict teaching style was what made the course content very challenging. One day in the beginning of the semester, after explaining a concept in class, he suddenly said, "Eighteen point two percent."

We students looked at him very confused. That number had nothing to do with what he had just explained. What was he talking about? Well, I guess we were supposed to know the answer to that question because the next thing he said was, "What does that number mean?"

To my surprise, after a moment of silence, one of my classmates said, "That's the percentage of us who understood what you just explained."

One of Dr. James's previous students must have told that to my classmate, because there was no way for us to even imagine that a random number was the percentage of students who understood the content explained in class.

"Yes, exactly," Dr. James said. "Only eighteen point two percent of all of you understood what I just explained. And eighteen point two percent includes those of you who kind of understood it and those of you who understood it for a very short period of time but don't understand it anymore. So what does it tell you?"

It tells us that you should reteach that concept, I answered his question in my mind. Everybody seemed to have silently answered that question too. That was probably a good thing, because I'm sure nobody would have come up with the answer the professor wanted to hear.

"That number says that you should think more about that concept. Read more about it. Talk about it in your study groups. Or find the eighteen point two percent of students who understood it and ask them to explain it to you." That was Dr. James's answer to his own question.

Dr. James didn't give us a percentage as an assessment of our learning in every class, but I'm sure if he did, it would never get to 100 percent. His classes were always delivered in a lecture style, rarely using the blackboard or anything else that could help students understand the statistics concepts. As a result, most students, native and nonnative English speakers, recorded his lectures so that we could listen to them later. It was actually good that many students were taping his lectures because if, for some reason, something happened to our recording, we could get it from someone else in class. I experienced that benefit one day. In one of the recorded lectures, Dr. James said, "OK, here's what you should know about path analysis." I immediately had my paper and pencil ready to take notes about what he was going to say next. Unfortunately, somehow the next few minutes of the lecture were not recorded. When I finally found the rest of the lecture that was recorded,

I listened to Dr. James saying, "So that's what you should know about path analysis." I couldn't believe that the most important part of the class hadn't been recorded! Fortunately, I had about twenty other classmates who could give me the recording of the lecture.

It was helpful to record Dr. James's lectures, but it was also time consuming, especially because of the thousands of notes I would have to take while listening to the audio. Dr. James encouraged us to study in groups. That again was very helpful but also time consuming. I met with my study group twice a week for about three hours—not including the time that I spent on the assignments for this course. The bottom line is that many other students and I basically realized in the beginning of the semester that we would have to teach ourselves everything that was explained in class, and that was going to take a lot of our time.

In short, at the end of my first week of classes, when I was finally back home in Houston for a few days, I sat down to create my to-do list for the following week. As I examined my endless to-do list and everything else that I would need to get done in that semester, I thought, *How am I going to get all this done? If I'm not careful, I will easily get stressed throughout the semester. And I bet I will have several cold sores.* Cold sores were already part of my life. Since I was a teenager, I've had a cold sore every time I am stressed or anxious about something. As soon as I turned my attention to cold sores, I stopped myself before those thoughts resulted in a cold sore right there and then, even before the actual stress started.

I said to myself, "This is my chance to test if everything that I learned from Paulo Vieira (e.g., strategies for an extraordinary life) and Shawn Achor (e.g., brain exercises) really works for me." With that in mind, in addition to focusing on the positive vision of my future and the fact that I didn't want to go back to being the Angelica from before my new-me journey, I decided to find time to keep exercising, journaling, writing down three things I was grateful for, doing an act of kindness, and going over the goals I had created for each component of the circle of life.

Feeding Your Mind

While putting into practice the strategies I had learned, I kept watching YouTube videos to build on the knowledge I had already gained about improving my life. There were many YouTube videos on self-improvement, motivation, and success. I then chose to watch videos of Tony Robbins, an American author, entrepreneur, and life coach. I selected his videos because I had heard that his work resonated with the strategies I was practicing.

Robbins's ideas mainly reinforced the ones I was already putting into practice. His lectures encouraged me even more to believe in myself and try my hardest to achieve my goals. It was very motivating to listen to encouraging words every day and be reminded that changes happen fast. However, we need to *want to* change and take action to actually change it.

Robbins's work was mainly significant to me for two reasons. First, he said that one important thing we had to do if we wanted to change or improve something in our lives was to feed our minds with knowledge about it.[21] That tip told me I was doing the right thing by watching YouTube videos every single day to learn more about how to improve my life.

You must be wondering when I had time to watch the videos, since I had already started a busy academic semester. Well, since I didn't have time to dedicate exclusively to them, I paired up some of my everyday routines with the videos. I would listen to them while driving, walking, exercising, and having lunch by myself. It was definitely enough time to feed my mind so well to the point that I was highly motivated to focus

---

21. Robbins, "Feed Your Mind."

on my work and confident that I could face any challenge that might come.

The second reason why Robbins's work was significant to me was that he made me realize what I was looking for all this time: happiness.

Defining Happiness

Robbins's work served as a bridge that finally connected my new-me journey to what I was actually looking for: happiness. Looking for new videos of Robbins to watch, I came across one that caught my attention. It was called "The Secret of Happiness." Until that day, many things were still unclear to me. There I was listening to those videos every day to learn how to improve my life and reach my goals. But exactly what did I want to improve about my life? What goals did I have in life besides completing my PhD and getting a job as a professor?

In that video, Robbins defined happiness as *progress*—that is, actions that lead to growth make us happy. He went on to say, "Whenever you feel happy in an area of your life, it's because your current life experience, that is, life conditions in that area, match or exceed your beliefs about how life should be in that area."[22] For example, some people might feel happy with their career because they have achieved the job position they expected to reach.

Using the questioning strategy, Robbins encouraged us to ask ourselves, "What is an area in your life that you feel proud and happy about?"[23] As I thought about that question, I immediately said to myself, "I feel proud and happy about my professional life," which at the moment also includes my academic life. My doctoral course grades, compliments from my adviser, invitations for research collaboration, and evaluations from my undergraduate students and professors for whom

---

22. Robbins, "The Secret of Happiness."
23. Ibid.

I had worked showed that I was doing a good job and all my hard work was worthwhile. All that recognition made me feel proud and happy about my current professional life, especially when I compared it with my previous professional life experiences. Allow me to share a couple of personal stories, so you can better understand the comparison between my current and previous professional life experiences.

When I think about some of the places I have worked, I remember feeling stuck careerwise. I felt like someone was holding me back by my shirt. Although I was already being the best teacher I could be, my desire was to do more for the English-language-learner population. I wanted to grow professionally, but my opportunities for growth were very limited because public education comes with many rules and expectations for teachers and students. Knowing that I wanted to grow in my career and that my professional skills were not being used to the fullest made me feel frustrated and stuck in a place where all I could do was follow rules and expectations.

When I think about some of the places where I have worked, I also remember not feeling valued or known for who I am. I felt like I had another identity. Even after I introduced myself clearly by saying, "My name is Angelica. I'm from Brazil, and Portuguese is my first language," many of my coworkers still thought my name was pronounced AnHelica, I was from Mexico, and Spanish was my first language.

One day a teacher came to my classroom with a student who spoke Spanish as a first language and said, "Could you please call his mother to say he forgot his homework again?"

Confused, I asked, "What?" I didn't understand why *I* had to call a student's parent when he was not even *my* student. *I bet it's because the student's mother doesn't speak English and the teacher thinks I speak Spanish*, I thought.

He clarified, "His mother doesn't speak English."

Bingo! I thought. It was no surprise anymore to be seen as a Spanish speaker. Since this event happened before my new-me journey, you can guess what I did. "Yes. Sure, I can call her. What's the number?" I asked. Now, you may be thinking that I speak Spanish fluently. I don't. But at the time, I had such an instinct of saying *yes* that I would even forget that I only knew enough Spanish to get by (because Portuguese has a lot of similarities with Spanish). Anyway, I used my made-up Mexican identity and managed to call the student's mother to let her know about the homework.

There were many other times when my coworkers thought I spoke Spanish. One day, a lady (who, by the way, was just replacing someone else for the day) started telling me a story in English, and all of a sudden, she continued her story in Spanish. What made her think I could understand Spanish? She had never seen me before, and I didn't even introduce myself to her before she started with the story. But there she was, already assuming that my made-up identity actually belonged to me. This event also happened before my new-me journey, which means that yes, despite understanding the story, I never stopped her to say, "I'm sorry to interrupt, but I don't speak Spanish. Could you please speak English?" I simply let her keep thinking that I spoke Spanish and was probably from Mexico.

One day as I talked with my grandma about when she was in the hospital with pneumonia, she said, "You know, I can't remember being in the hospital. Instead, I have the impression that I was away on a trip."

"Really, Grandma? It's actually good that you don't remember being in the hospital. Where were you in the trip you think you took?"

"In Mexico," she answered. I laughed, especially because I had never told her about the Mexican identity that some coworkers had given me.

Let's go back for a minute to Robbins's question: "What is an area in your life that you feel proud and happy about?"[24] As I said, I am

24. Ibid.

definitely proud and happy with my current professional life. At Texas A&M University, I am not only known for who I am, but I am also being challenged with coursework and research projects, which give me the feeling of growth. Following Robbins's logic of happiness, since feeling valued and challenged match my expectations and beliefs, I feel happy with my current professional life.

"Is there any other area in my life where I feel proud and happy?" I asked myself. I forced myself to say I feel happy with Kent, which was true, but not always. So would it count? Could I answer that question referring to someone who *many times*, but not *always*, makes me feel happy? Since Robbins wasn't there to answer me, I just decided *no*. If I wanted to say that Kent made me happy, it would have to be more than many times. It doesn't mean that I didn't love him. I did and *do* love him a lot! Kent is a kind, caring, smart, considerate person whom I feel blessed to share my life with. But there were times that our differences would cause me not to feel 100 percent happy with him. For example, I am very organized; Kent is not as organized, although his organizational skills have improved a lot since we got married. (It must have been a social-contagion effect.) I am very committed to getting things done right away so that I can check them off my to-do list; Kent has a hard time even making a to-do list, and it doesn't bother him to get things done at the last minute. I am an introvert; he is an extrovert. I don't like to watch much TV; he loves to watch TV. I am very careful with money; he is not as careful. These differences would then lead to some disagreements, which would affect my happiness with him.

I kept asking myself, "Is there anything else that I am doing well and, therefore, feeling happy about it? Family? No. Friends? No. Fitness? Yes. Good! At least I found one more area in my life about which I am completely happy." I have been constantly exercising and eating healthily. Again, like my current career, my fitness matches my expectations and beliefs. So no wonder I was feeling happy about it.

Robbins's next question was, "What is an area in your life that you are *not* happy with?"[25] My relationship with Kent was the first thought that came to my mind. As I said before, I was happy with him, but I wanted to be *constantly* happy with him. I wanted to find out how I could avoid our differences getting in the way of my happiness. (It didn't seem that our differences bothered him; he was constantly happy.)

Family and social connections were the second thought that came to my mind when I considered areas in my life that didn't make me 100 percent happy. Since I started putting into practice the circle-of-life goals, I was feeling a lot better about staying in touch with family and friends. But I still needed to improve my social connections.

Moving to Houston meant making new friends. At first, most of the friends I made here were because of Kent's extroverted personality. For example, one day after we first moved to Houston, we were on our way back from putting our trash away at the apartment complex when we saw a man and woman talking. Since I didn't know them, I would have just greeted them with a smile and walked away. But not Kent—he stopped them with the excuse that he thought they were talking to him. They were not. So Kent said, "Sorry, I thought you were talking to me. By the way, I'm Kent. This is my wife, Angelica."

"Hi, I'm Mary, and this is Tom," the woman said.

"Do you guys live here?" Kent asked them. Two minutes later, we found out that Mary was our neighbor and worked at the same university as Kent. That led to twenty more minutes of talk. Today, I am very grateful that we decided to take the trash out that evening, at that time, and that Kent initiated the conversation, because Mary and I have become good friends since then.

I have tried to make friends on my own too. After moving to Houston, I thought it would be easier to make friends at work, since I

25. Ibid.

would often be in touch with my coworkers. Well, it wasn't that easy. Maybe coffee could help, I decided.

As an attempt to make a new friend, I decided to use a move that I had already noticed other Americans successfully using: invite someone to get together for coffee. Now, remember this was before my new-me journey, meaning that, besides being an introvert, I wasn't assertive or confident. So to take the initiative to invite an acquaintance or coworker for coffee took some effort on my part. But I was determined to make new friends.

One day I took advantage of a professional-development day we had at school to test my "move" with one of the teachers.

"Hi!" I greeted her with a smile.

"Oh, hi."

"I'm glad the professional-development workshop finished earlier than expected so that we can work alone in our classrooms."

"I know. Me too."

"Listen, since we rarely have the chance to leave school during work hours, I'm going to quickly grab some coffee at Starbucks and then come back. Would you like to come?"

"No, thank you. I don't drink coffee."

"Oh, OK then," I said disappointedly.

Maybe she didn't want to come because she had a lot to do in her class-room, I thought, looking for a better excuse than "I don't drink coffee."

A few months later, I invited another coworker for coffee. "Sorry, I can't drink coffee. It makes me sick," she said.

Maybe I should start inviting them to have some tea, I thought.

Again, months later, still trying to make a new friend, I approached a different coworker. "Would you like to get together this weekend?" I asked her, making sure to leave the coffee item out of the invitation.

"Sure," she answered without hesitation.

"Great! So I will call you on the weekend to set the place and time," I said excitedly, thinking, *I guess coffee was what was holding me back from making plans to get together with a potential friend.* Or maybe not. The weekend came. I called her. I left her a message. She never called me back. She didn't say anything about it at work either, until I went to her classroom to say hi. She then apologized and said that a family member had had a small accident over the weekend. She didn't offer to reschedule our get-together, nor did I because I didn't want to be seen as someone who was insisting too much on hanging out with her.

Here's my favorite story about trying to make a new friend. One day when I had just moved to Houston and was still unfamiliar with the area, one of my coworkers made me think for a few seconds that *she* was actually the one trying to make a new friend. After telling her I had moved to Houston just a few weeks before, she asked, "Do you know where the mall is?"

"No, I don't."

"Oh, whenever you want to go there, call me and…"

Before she even finished her sentence, I thought, *Oh, great! Instead of inviting someone to get together, someone is actually going to invite me to hang out. She does seem nice. It'll be very good to have a new friend, especially in a city where Kent and I have no family or friends yet.*

"…and I will tell you how to get there," she completed her sentence.

What? I thought. *"Call me and I will tell you how to get there?" Was that what she really said?* I doubted my English skills for a second. Yes, I was right. That's what she said. I have to confess that was not what I expected to hear. But after all the noes that I received from the coffee invitations, I wasn't really surprised. I appreciated that she wanted to help me, but hadn't she heard of GPS or Google Maps? It's been a while since I used a paper map or asked someone for directions.

A few years later, I ran into a former coworker at the gym. After greeting her and quickly catching up on what we were doing for work, she said, "Let's exchange phone numbers so that we can get together for coffee someday."

Wow! Someone is inviting me for coffee? I thought. By then, I had given up on the idea of trying to make friends by inviting them to get together. Anyway, I wasn't sure if that potential coffee would lead us to friendship. But without hesitation (especially because I didn't want her to feel what I felt after inviting people to have coffee), I excitedly said, "Oh, yes. Definitely! I'd love to have coffee with you someday."

We exchanged contact information. A few weeks later, I contacted her to schedule our coffee get-together. On the day that we had planned to meet, I texted her to say that I was going to be a few minutes late.

"Late for what?" she replied.

"For our coffee," I texted her back.

"Oh, I'm sorry. I completely forgot about it."

My original thought of *Wow! Someone is inviting me for coffee?* turned into *Oh, well, I guess sometimes I should stop trying something and just let it happen naturally.* I was right. Since then, without any effort, I have become friends with people who I met through my PhD program, family members, and old friends. Now it's up to me to maintain these new friendships.

Thinking about Robbins's questions regarding the areas in my life that I feel happy or unhappy about made me realize what it takes for us to be happy: action! I am happy with my current career and fitness because I am taking actions to make those two areas match my life expectations and beliefs. Based on my life expectations and beliefs, I needed to have a relationship with Kent that would make me feel happier to be with him and to keep in touch with my family members and friends. Therefore, to be happier with Kent and my social connections, I needed to take actions that would be aligned with the beliefs and expectations I had for my relationship with Kent and social connections.

My new-me journey was already encouraging me to act in order to match my actions toward my life expectations and beliefs. For example, following my *relationship with my significant other* circle-of-life goal, every day I made sure to compliment, spend quality time, or have a conversation with Kent; following my *social* and *family* circle-of-life goals, every day I either sent a text message, called, or went out with a friend or family member. Thinking about all the actions (from the circle-of-life goals and brain exercises) that I had already added to my routine, I realized that my new-me journey was actually leading me beyond self-improvement; it was leading me to happiness.

Until then, I believed that happiness was something that would naturally come into our lives after big events or accomplishments (e.g., school graduation), but without us mindfully putting too much effort into being happy. It had never occurred to me that happiness could be a result of meaningful actions—actions that would make me grow so that I would align my beliefs and expectations to my current life experiences. As I reflected on *happiness*, I concluded, "Yes! It *is* happiness that I was looking for in order to improve myself as a person. Now, I need to learn more about it."

WHAT ABOUT YOU?

- *What is an area in your life that you feel happy about? What actions are you taking to feel happy in that area?*
- *What is an area in your life that you don't feel happy about? What actions can you take in order to feel happy about that area?*

Four

LEARNING MORE ABOUT HAPPINESS

I typed *happiness* on YouTube and clicked on search. I was immediately overwhelmed with so many videos that came out as a result of that search. Which one should I watch? One of the first ones was "Don't Worry, Be Happy Now: The Science and Philosophy of the Happiness Movement with Gretchen Rubin," an interview with Rubin about her book *The Happiness Project*. *The Happiness Project*? I was immediately intrigued by the title of her book. I had never seen the word *project* being used with *happiness*. I had seen *science project, school project, class project*, and other types of hands-on activities that we usually refer to as a project because it requires concrete materials to create something. But *happiness project* I had never heard before. What concrete materials would people use to create the abstract feeling of happiness? My curiosity dragged my finger to click on that video.

The more I listened to Rubin talking about her happiness project, the more I liked her perspective. She seemed to have a practical approach toward happiness, which resonated with me. For example, she mentioned that she kept a checklist with resolutions she had set for herself.[26] Since

---

26. Rubin, interview, "Don't Worry, Be Happy Now."

I love checklists, I liked her approach already. She also mentioned that when she asked people what was one habit that boosted their happiness, they said it was to make the bed as soon as they got up. "Make the bed?" I was as surprised as everybody else who was watching the interview live. Even still not understanding why making the bed would have a positive impact on many people's lives, I was immediately grateful for my mother asking me to make the bed every day (since I was a little girl—literally little because I remember not even being able to fold my sheet by myself due to my little arms)—a habit that I still have today. Because making the bed is somehow associated with happiness, I wondered if my other habits were related to happiness as well. "Could the habit of wiping and organizing the desk before I actually sit down to do my work have any correlation to happiness?" I asked myself.

As I continued listening to Rubin, more of her ideas resonated with me. When asked what she would recommend people do to change addictions they might have, such as constantly using their smartphones, she said that people should have boundaries.[27] For instance, people should set time to work without interruptions, including the ones coming from their phones. As an example, she said that she removed the notifications from her phone and never had the ringer on, in order to avoid being interrupted. As a result, she was more productive, which led her to feel happier because of her accomplishments.

This time, I wasn't surprised to hear that the phone ringer was off, but to have the notifications off (including those from e-mails and text messages), *that* surprised me. It is going to sound silly, but the first thought that came to my mind was, *Are we even allowed to turn off notifications from text messages? Don't we get a fine or some kind of punishment for doing that?* This new technology era we live in has come to a point that it seems we frequently have to be available to people who contact us. For example, one day I saw a notification on my phone letting

---

27. Ibid.

me know that a cousin of mine had sent a text. Since I was studying, I didn't check the message right at that moment. Not even ten minutes later, I received another notification letting me know that the same cousin had sent another text message. Because I could see the first lines of the message, I saw several question marks. Confused, I decided to stop my reading to open the text. "*????*" That's all her second text said, which I interpreted as "Hello? Angeeeelica! Are you there? Why don't you answer me? Are you busy? Why don't you check your messages?" or simply "Hurry up!" Then I checked her first text because the question marks implied it could be something urgent. Not really, at least not in my opinion. The first text asked me to translate a sentence from Portuguese to English. Trying to distract my thought of *I can't believe that I interrupted my studies for this*, I practiced my gratitudes by saying to myself that I was feeling honored to have been chosen as a translator over Google Translator.

Anyway, my point is that many times, we are not only interrupted by text messages but also expected to reply right away. Such expectation, then, makes texts a bigger distraction, especially when we are working or studying. With that said, inspired by Rubin, I turned off the text-message notifications from my phone.

Rubin also mentioned that she scheduled a weekly hangout time with her older daughter.[28] Both of them had busy schedules, so to make sure they spent quality time together, they did something fun for about two hours every week. That reminded me of my weekly phone calls to my grandma, uncle, and aunt.

My grandma is ninety-four years old, but mentally and physically, she doesn't seem to be ninety-four at all. As long as I can remember, I have always been very close to her. It was probably because her house served as a daycare and after-school program for me—not including all the times I went there for parties and visits. When I moved to the

---

28. Ibid.

United States, I would randomly call her. Then, as a way to spend more time with my grandma, I decided to call her once a week. Our phone calls make the two of us very happy!

Unfortunately, in 2013, my uncle Fontenele found out that he had pancreatic cancer. It seemed like a nightmare when I was first told about it. I found myself helpless. I wanted to help him somehow but couldn't. I was not even able to be with him, since I live so far away. That was when I decided to call him and his wife every week as well. Since then, we have not only kept in touch with each other's lives, but we also have grown closer.

Going back to Rubin, as she talked about her happiness project, it was clear that her book portrayed happiness through productivity, habits, routines, and social connections—everything that interested me.[29] By the end of the interview, I decided to buy her book *The Happiness Project.*

I chose to buy the audiobook, knowing there wouldn't be time to read extra books besides the ones I was already assigned in my graduate courses. This decision actually came at a good time because at the end of the last two months, Kent and the phone company reminded me that my cellular data plan had already been used up. It was definitely because of all the YouTube videos I listened to during my trips going back and forth between Houston and College Station. So I did need a backup plan in order to keep learning about happiness during my "free time."

The Happiness Project audiobook was my backup plan, and the more I listened about how Rubin was able to incorporate more happiness into her everyday life, the more I wanted to learn about happiness. I enjoyed the book so much that even before I finished it, I decided to create my own happiness project.

Besides being inspired by Rubin's successful happiness project and having the desire to be happier in life, I wanted to create my own happiness project for two eye-opening reasons that Rubin mentioned: experiencing the advantages of being a happy person and becoming ready

---

29. Ibid.

to handle difficult moments. Based on research, she said that "happy people are more altruistic, more productive, more helpful, more likable, more creative, more resilient, more interested in others, friendlier, and healthier. Happy people make better friends, colleagues, and citizens."[30] In addition to all that, because of the social-contagion effect, happy people boost the happiness of those around them.

The other eye-opening reason for me to pursue happiness was to be ready to handle difficult moments—"to develop the self-discipline and the mental habits to deal with the bad thing when it happened," Rubin said.[31] She went on to remind us not to wait for a crisis to happen so that we could change something in our lives. As she said, the phone is going to ring, and we should be prepared to face whatever reality it brings.[32] I completely agreed with her, especially because I had already experienced those phone calls or messages. In 2008, I received an e-mail saying that my paternal grandmother had passed away. In 2013, I got a call informing me about my uncle's pancreatic cancer. In 2015, I received a text message telling me that my maternal grandmother was in the hospital with pneumonia. With all that in mind and without any hesitation, I decided to create my own happiness project. That was when I changed my new-me journey to my happiness journey.

A few days later, I e-mailed Rubin to let her know she had inspired me to create my own project.

Dear Gretchen Rubin,

I am writing to you to say thank you for sharing your ideas on how to be happy. I recently bought your book The Happiness Project (I know, you

---

30. Rubin, *The Happiness Project*, Getting Started.
31. Ibid.
32. Ibid.

wrote it years ago, but just now I came across it) and it has already helped me A LOT. I haven't finished the book yet, but by what I have read and learned about you through YouTube videos and Podcasts, I find that we have a lot in common. So your book has been an inspiration to me because if your resolutions to achieve happiness worked for you, they might work for me too.

Like you, I am an upholder [this term will be explained in chapter 5], like to follow schedules, love to make and commit to to-do lists, find myself boring at times because I am so committed to my work, eat the same things every day, and want to find (I should actually say improve) happiness right here where I am (Houston, TX) as I follow my everyday routine.

With that said, thank you for opening my eyes to a new perspective on happiness. Being a PhD student, my time is very limited, but you have showed me that I can find happiness in little things that I do in my everyday life. As an upholder, when I say I am going to do something, I really commit to it (so, many times I have to think twice before I make a commitment :)). I have decided to create and implement my own commandments and resolutions to improve my happiness. Thanks for inspiring me!

Best wishes,
Angelica

A few weeks later, when I routinely checked my e-mails, I saw an e-mail from Rubin. I could barely believe she had taken time to e-mail a stranger back. I was so happy! Here's what she wrote:

```
Hi Angelica,

Thanks so much for your kind email. I'm thrilled
to hear that my work resonates with you.
I very much appreciate you taking the time to
write.

Warmly,
Gretchen
```

I decided to tell Rubin about my decision to create my own happiness project, because knowing myself, if I told someone about it, I would follow it through. And I did. Soon after I finished listening to her book, I created *my commandments* and *resolutions*—two main guiding tools of her happiness project.

Commandments

According to Rubin's happiness project, we should set our own commandments to represent the principles that guide our lives.[33] The commandments are supposed to remind us of what we believe in and how we should act; therefore, they should also help us get through challenging moments.

After a lot of consideration, I finalized my commandments, some of which are inspired by Rubin's own commandments.[34]

---

33. Ibid.
34. Ibid.

My Commandments

1. Be Angelica.
2. Let it go.
3. Act the way I want to feel.
4. Enjoy the process.
5. Stay in touch.
6. Lighten up. Do something fun.
7. Just do it. Do it for *myself.*
8. Do good; feel good.
9. Don't give up.
10. Smile.
11. Listen.
12. Be assertive and confident. (It's OK to say no.)
13. Take advantage of the opportunities.
14. Don't judge. Be curious.
15. Be grateful.

Once I had completed my commandments, I had to find a way to revisit and keep them fresh in my mind. So I printed several copies of them on a yellow sheet of paper and spread them around the places where I mostly spent the week: the apartment where I stayed in College Station, my office at the university, and at home. I also considered the times when I would not be at any of those places, so I put a copy of my commandments in my planner, in my wallet, in the back of my cell phone, and on my computer. Being constantly surrounded by my commandments, I had no excuse not to remember the principles I wanted to live by in my daily life.

Having several little pieces of yellow paper around the house meant that I had to tell Kent about my commandments. He is a questioner, meaning that it would be a matter of minutes for him to ask, "What is it? What is it for? Where did you get it from?" To beat him to his questions, I told him not only about the commandments but also about my new-me journey, which turned into my happiness journey. I told him about what I had learned from Vieira, Achor, Robbins, and Rubin. I told him about what I had incorporated into my daily routine (such as the brain exercises and circle-of-life goals) to have a more positive and happier life.

Until then, I had shared my new journey (now called my happiness journey) only with Dr. Sarah. I hesitated telling Kent about my happiness journey because I was afraid that he would expect me to be positive and happy all the time. Sure enough! One day, when he noticed that I wasn't in my best mood, he reminded me of my happiness journey. He then implied I was supposed to be in a good mood because of the happy journey that I had decided to take. I immediately said, "Just because I decided to implement my happiness journey, it doesn't mean that I have to be happy all the time. I am not perfect! There will definitely be moments when I will feel upset and sad, and that will impact my mood."

After my explanation, I am sure Kent agreed with me because when he saw me feeling down other times after that day, he said to me, "You don't have to feel happy all the time. There are moments when we just feel sad, and that's OK."

Resolutions

Besides her commandments, Rubin's happiness project was also guided by resolutions, which were concrete goals that she wanted to accomplish in her daily life. After creating about five resolutions per month, she went through each of them at the end of the day. She put a check mark next to the ones that were accomplished and an X next to the ones that were not accomplished.[35]

---

35. Ibid.

Her resolutions idea reminded me of my circle-of-life goals that I was already practicing. Similar to her idea, I also created a list of concrete goals to review every night, to check the ones I had addressed that day. The circle of life included several components of life: *health, social, relationship with a significant other, family, spiritual, emotional, professional, financial, intellectual,* and *service.*[36] The difference between Rubin's resolutions and the circle-of-life goals is that the latter makes sure I addressed a goal for each component of life. Rubin also considered different aspects of life, but over one whole year, as opposed to daily. Her resolutions were based on a theme she had established for each month of the year. After each month, she would carry out the resolutions from the previous month to the next one and create new resolutions for the new month. As for my circle-of-life goals, I didn't change them, in order to keep the strategy simple.

Despite the fact that Rubin's resolution idea was similar to the circle-of-life goals, I decided to add her idea to my daily routine. Although no one would see my resolution checklist, simply going over that checklist at the end of the day would help me incorporate new habits that I needed in life. I didn't even wait for a new month to start my resolutions. At the very end of October, I started with the following resolutions: *be on time, be clear, sleep for at least six and a half hours,* and *write.* I chose to begin with those actions because they would benefit me right way.

BE ON TIME

As a Brazilian, I was not the most punctual person in the world. Although there are many exceptions, generally speaking, Brazilians are very flexible with time, unless they have a serious commitment, such as to teach a class, run a business meeting, or punch in at work. Brazilians seem to be even more flexible with punctuality when it comes to leisure. Here's an example to illustrate how the notion of punctuality works in

---

36. Vieira, "Coaching: Prosperidade de vida" (Coaching: Prosperity of Life).

the Brazilian culture. In the United States, parties usually have a clear time to start and end. In Brazil, when the host or hostess invites the guests, he or she usually says, "The party starts from eight o'clock on." What does that mean? Good question! That means that the guests start arriving at the party around eight thirty at the earliest! And if they arrive exactly at 8:00 p.m., they will surprise the host.

I remember being in elementary school, and one day after getting out of my father's car, a school staff member said to me, "You've been late to school several times now. I'll have to talk to your father about your tardiness."

Being as honest as a child can be, I replied, "But many times I am late because of him!"

She was speechless. That situation shows that, unfortunately, the Brazilian notion of punctuality passes on from generation to generation.

Since I moved to the United States, my punctuality had already improved a lot, but there was still room for improvement. For example, I would often be a few minutes late to my classes (not the classes that I taught, of course) or informal gatherings with friends. To my surprise, even before making this resolution, I had already noticed that simply being on time to my appointments would make me feel happy. Besides, when I was on time, I looked more responsible, prepared, and committed to the people I was meeting. So I made the resolution to be on time for all my appointments, no matter what they were.

It was easy to make the resolution of being on time, but it took me some time to have a clear understanding of what it meant to be on time. One day my watch showed that my philosophy class was going to start in five minutes. I needed to use the restroom, especially because the professor did not give us a break during his three-hour-long class. I decided to go straight to the classroom because I didn't want to be late. So I arrived at the classroom on time. The professor arrived right after me. After greeting him, I excused myself to use the restroom. On the way to the restroom, I thought, *Is that being on time?*

Another example of lack of clarity about being punctual happened when I rushed to be on time for a research meeting. I arrived at the meeting exactly at 1:00 p.m., the starting time. But this time the professor was running late. Realizing I had forgotten some materials for the meeting, I left the room to pick them up in my office. When I walked back into the room, the professor was there. *Is this being on time?* I asked myself.

There were also times when I was on my way to a class or meeting and I would end up arriving there late because a professor or colleague stopped me on the way. Then I would think, *I wouldn't have been late if I hadn't run into them. So is that being on time?*

With all those types of situations in mind, one day I finally decided to define what *being on time* meant to me. Here's the definition I created for myself: to be on time meant to be at least one minute early to my appointments and be fully prepared, that is, having all the necessary materials, not feeling hungry or needing to use the restroom. Creating this clear understanding of what it meant to be on time helped me implement this resolution. By simply arriving on time, I was feeling happier and showing how responsible, prepared, and committed I could be.

Be Clear

I applied the same concept of clarity to the resolution *be clear*. I chose this resolution because Kent would often say that I was not completely clear in expressing my ideas. After giving a lot of thought as to why I could be clear with friends and family from Brazil but not with Kent, I concluded it was probably a language issue (not in terms of language proficiency, but language use).

Different from native English speakers, Portuguese speakers tend to leave some words out of the sentences because they are implied in the conversation. For example, let's say that a friend said that he or she went to the movies. As a Portuguese speaker, I would be tempted to ask, "Did you like?" I would not think to add the object of the sentence, that is, the words *the movie* or *it* after the verb *like*, because the context of the conversation would imply I was referring to the movie. On the other hand, as an English speaker, Kent would ask, "Did you like the movie?" or "Did you like it?" making very clear that he was inquiring about the movie. Different from Portuguese, the English language is very explicit and direct. Also, Portuguese is a prolific language, meaning that many times we use a lot of words to make our point (which is ironic since, as mentioned above, Portuguese speakers tend to leave words out of the sentences because they are implied in the conversation).

Even though I started studying English in fifth grade, I was never explicitly taught about those differences between the use of English and Portuguese. English textbooks might not address the differences because they don't focus only on English learners who are Portuguese speakers or because they believe those are minor differences that won't really impact interactions between native and nonnative English speakers. Well, if the latter reason is the case, I would have to disagree with those textbook companies. During our ten-plus years of relationship, many times after listening to me going on and on about something, Kent would ask me, "OK, but what's your point?"

"Hold on. Let me tell you the full story first. Are you in a rush?" I would say.

He would patiently listen to me. When I would finally get to the point of my story, he would say, "You're so funny. You talk a lot to get to the main idea of what you want to share."

First, I didn't give much thought to Kent's reactions to my yada yada yada. I didn't give much attention to all the times when he interrupted me to ask for clarification, which was usually about particular information I omitted from the sentences. However, one day Kent said, "You know, you should speak clearer, especially now that you have to give presentations at the university and conferences." I kept his words in mind and, through interactions with other people, I started to realize he was right: I had to be clearer when speaking. I had to be mindful about not letting the Portuguese language influence the clarity of what I said in English. To *be clear* in English to me meant to start my talk with the main point and make sure to use complete sentences.

Now, you might be wondering what the resolution to *be clear* has to do with happiness. Well, it is connected to happiness mainly through my interactions with Kent. Due to my lack of clarity, there would be times when our conversations would end in frustration, which would then affect my mood and impact our relationship. Therefore, it was important that I resolved to be clear. That resolution would not only contribute to my relationship with Kent, but it would also help me become a better graduate student, instructor, and English speaker.

SLEEP FOR AT LEAST SIX AND A HALF HOURS

Sleep for at least six and a half hours was another resolution I set for myself. Six and a half hours doesn't seem like much, but it was a reasonable amount compared to how long I was sleeping at the time (an average of five hours per night, including on weekends). I definitely needed to sleep more, but with everything I had to accomplish for the three courses I was taking as a student and two that I was teaching, I wrongly prioritized my working hours. I stayed up late working and got up early to work. However, after listening to Achor's audiobook *Before Happiness*, I was convinced that, different from what many people think, I could actually accomplish more by sleeping more. In Achor's words, "If you want to be able to see the details that will help your brain summon its full range of intellectual and emotional resources, first make sure you get seven to eight hours of sleep a night."[37] He added that lack of

---

37. Achor, *Before Happiness*, Skill 1, Gaining Perspective in Your Sleep section.

enough sleep makes our brains tired, which leads us to see fixed, negative reality.[38]

Additionally, as Rubin reminded us in her book *The Happiness Project*, lack of sleep can negatively affect our physical energy and happiness. She went on to say that "sleep deprivation impairs memory, weakens the immune system, slows metabolism, and might, some studies suggest, foster weight gain."[39]

Based on all those arguments in favor of a good night of sleep, I had no doubt that I needed to increase my number of sleeping hours. As a result, sleep would help me make good decisions, find solutions to problems, analyze situations through a positive reality, be healthier, and feel happier and more energetic. Moreover, sleep could indirectly improve my relationships and work and academic performance. Besides, I was starting to think that having a good night of sleep was Kent's biggest secret to his happiness. He frequently sleeps for about eight hours per night. So maybe that's why he is always in a good mood, quickly thinks of solutions, and has a positive view on things. That said, I decided to sleep at least six and a half hours every night, as I worked my way up to seven and then eight hours of sleep.

WRITE

To *write* was the fourth resolution I created. This resolution was inspired by Goodson's book *Becoming an Academic Writer*. Goodson reminded us of the important role of practice in developing new skills, such as writing. Based on the works of the psychologist K. Anders Ericsson, the neuroscientist George Bartzokis, and the author of *The Talent Code*, Daniel Coyle, she emphasized that deliberate practice was the key to acquire new skills and stated that "practice allows us to fire specific circuits in our brains repeatedly and to develop more myelin, the substance

---

38. Ibid.
39. Rubin, *The Happiness Project*, Chapter 1.

insulating the axons (or nerve fiber extensions of our neurons). In turn, more myelin leads to faster or more optimal firing of circuits and developing of skills."[40]

Since writing is a requirement in almost everything I do as a doctoral student, I could really benefit from the increase of myelin in my brain to help me improve my writing skills. So I resolved to write every day. By improving my writing, I would increase my academic performance and, consequently, it would boost my happiness.

FINAL THOUGHTS ON RESOLUTIONS

In December, I added new resolutions as I carried out the first four to my routine as well. Guided by my own commandments, my new resolutions were: *speak up, initiate a conversation, read for pleasure*, and *give compliments*. I chose those particular resolutions because they would increase my assertiveness, self-esteem, and happiness. Speaking up and initiating conversations would help me put my twelfth commandment (*Be assertive and confident*) into practice. Reading for pleasure would help me with my sixth commandment (*Lighten up. Do something fun*) and encourage me to read some books I had been wanting to finish for a while. And by complimenting people, I would not only make others feel good and important, but I would also feel good, which goes with what my eighth commandment says: *do good; feel good.*

As Rubin suggested, I went over my resolution list every night to check the ones I did and put an X next to the ones I didn't do that day.[41] At the end of the month, I went one step further and calculated the percentage frequency of each resolution to have clear results of which resolutions were becoming regular habits and which ones had to be reinforced.

---

40. Goodson, *Becoming an Academic Writer*, 8.
41. Rubin, *The Happiness Project*, Getting Started.

The implementation of those resolutions contributed tremendously to my happiness level. Many people (including *my old me*) tend to believe that happiness comes in big packages, such as a job promotion, the purchase of a car, or a trip to Hawaii. However, my resolutions made me realize that happiness can be wrapped in little packages called habits. Now I understand when Rubin said that *making the bed in the morning* makes a lot of people happy.[42] Many times, we may not even know that these little habits can make us happy; therefore, as a result of setting and committing to resolutions, we get to know ourselves better (in terms of what makes us happy) and bring happiness into our everyday lives.

Spiritual Master

Rubin also inspired me to adopt a spiritual master. According to her, our spiritual master should be someone whose traits and attitudes we not only admire but also someone whose traits and attitudes we may want to see in ourselves.[43] Our spiritual master can be a saint, an actor or actress, a teacher, a writer, a family member, or a friend. It doesn't matter if our spiritual master is famous or not, alive or not. The main purpose of having a spiritual master is for us to imitate him or her in order to strengthen our attitudes and ways of thinking, especially when facing challenging situations. As I read Rubin's work, I started to wonder who I could have as my spiritual master. The answer came when Rubin said that "spiritual people are happier; they are more mentally and physically healthier, feel better with stress, have better marriages, and live longer."[44] She added that spiritual people appreciate what they have and live in the present moment.[45] That's all I needed to realize that Grandma Margarida is and has always been my spiritual master.

---

42. Rubin, interview, "Don't Worry, Be Happy Now."
43. Rubin, *The Happiness Project*, Chapter 8.
44. Ibid.
45. Ibid.

Grandma Margarida, who is ninety-four years old, is happy and mentally and physically healthy, knows how to avoid stress, and had a great marriage. I grew up going to her house almost every day. Unfortunately, nowadays I visit her only once or twice a year when I go to Brazil. But as a way to spend more time with my grandma, I call her every single week at a set day and time. I am grateful that the technological advances allow us to see each other when we have our weekly long conversations. (Remember that Portuguese is a prolific language.)

Grandma Margarida appreciates what she has, no matter what it is. For example, not too long ago, I learned that she appreciated her old box TV very much, as opposed to a slim TV. After receiving a slim TV as a gift, she said to me, "I really liked my old TV because I could put stuff on top of it, but I can't do that with this new one. It's so thin that I can't put anything on it."

During our conversations, she often reminds me of how grateful she is for everything she has and for everything that has happened in her life, such as completing school and working as an accountant at a time when few women were hired. She also appreciates the challenging moments she has faced in life. Although she lives in the present moment, she enjoys sharing her life stories. For example, one day, a long time ago, since she and my grandfather didn't have much money, they had to choose between buying a fridge or a telephone. Both items were new to them. Having a hard time deciding on which one would be more useful, they decided to make an effort to purchase both of them. She was very happy not to have to run to the market every day to buy fresh food because now she had a fridge to preserve it.

As mentioned in chapter 1, Achor recommended journaling as a strategy to teach our minds to think positively.[46] He said journaling about a positive experience that happened to us makes us relive that situation. As a result, journaling boosts our happiness because it brings

---

46. Achor, "The Happy Secret to Better Work."

back the same good feelings we had when the positive experience happened. That is definitely true. Just by sharing stories with me, it was amazing to see how much happier my grandma felt. I love listening to her stories because, besides learning about her life, they make her feel happier, which makes me happy.

Grandma Margarida also knows how to avoid stress very well. She does that by interpreting life situations through positive lenses. She often says there are two interpretations for every situation: the good one and the bad one. "It's up to us to interpret the situation through a positive or negative perspective," she says. Grandma doesn't only lecture about good attitudes; she practices good attitudes. Here's an example of how she interpreted a situation through a positive perspective. She told me that when her sons and daughters were still very young (by the way, I should mention she had twelve children), one of her very good friends, Julieta, got married and didn't invite her to the wedding. But, strangely enough, the next day, Julieta's grandmother invited my grandma to her house to talk about the party and see her granddaughter's wedding gifts. Instead of feeling upset or disappointed with her close friend for not being invited to the wedding, Grandma used her Pollyanna way of thinking. She said to me, "I'm sure Julieta didn't invite me to her wedding because she knew I had many young children, so it would cost me money and time to get all of them nicely dressed for the wedding." (Grandma Margarida made her children's clothes.) "Also, I would have to buy a wedding gift, and she knew we didn't have much money. Not to mention the transportation to take my whole family to the wedding. With all that, I was happy not to be invited for her wedding. I actually ended up with the best part: having a nice conversation with her grandmother as we looked at the wedding gifts."

Stories like that one, in which my grandma was able to see a positive reality, happen daily in her life. I think that is what makes her such a strong and happy woman. Not too long ago, while many of my relatives were trying to cope with the pain of seeing someone we love in the hospital, in a very composed way, Grandma said, "You know, God allows us to be sick so that we have the opportunity to reflect on our lives, think about the good things we have done, and what we should improve about our lives."

My grandma's positive attitudes and thinking are so inspiring that I have made a list of life lessons based on the stories that she shared with me in our weekly phone calls. I compiled her life lessons in a booklet and made 150 bookmarks (one with each lesson) to be her ninety-fourth birthday party favor. Some of her life lessons are as follows:

- *"We should think of happy and funny things."*
- *"Don't get upset about silly things."*
- *"Everything we do goes away, except for the goodness we do to others."*
- *"We create our own happiness."*
- *"The first thing we should do is to love ourselves."*
- *"Don't be afraid. Be brave!"*
- *"Everything has the right time to happen. Just be patient."*

Those are some life lessons from someone who was born in 1922 in a small village in the northeast of Brazil, where there was no electricity or running water. Yet, she says that if she could restart her whole life, she would want to be born in 1922 in the same small village and have twelve children with my grandfather all over again. That's my grandma Margarida, a wise woman who has inspired me and many other people with her kindness and positive attitudes, which are reflected in her constant and genuine happy smile. She is my spiritual master.

Reactions about Happiness

Rubin's happiness project greatly impacted my life as she taught me that, among other things, I could create happiness by following my own commandments, meaningful resolutions, and spiritual master.[47] I was so inspired by Rubin that happiness became a topic in my conversations while I tried to find people to create a happiness group, as she suggested at the end of her book. I knew that social media could take me to people who shared my same interest. But I was trying to have a face-to-face happiness group with people I already knew. Assuming that happiness is everybody's ultimate goal, I thought it was going to be easy to find at least two other people to start a happiness group. To my surprise, it was not easy to find them. Actually, I'm still looking for them.

I was amazed to even see the reactions of some of my friends when I brought up the topic of happiness. They showed surprise and lack of interest in the topic. Their reactions were unexpected to me because everybody seems to want to be happy. Yet, when the word *happiness* comes up in the conversation, it sounds like it is an unfamiliar, strange word. Here are some examples of my attempts to talk about happiness with some friends. One day, during my break from coursework, I asked a friend who was also in graduate school, "What makes you happy?"

"What?" she asked with a confused look on her face, as if she was trying to make sense of what I had asked.

"What makes you *happy*?" I repeated, emphasizing the word *happy*.

Without much thought, as she got ready to leave the office, she said, "Getting this work done," referring to an article she was working on. She didn't seem to be interested in talking about happiness.

Some days later, I asked another graduate-school friend, "Are you happy?"

"What?" she asked with the same confused look I had seen on my other friend's face.

So I repeated my question, "Are you *happy*?"

"Why? Why would I be happy? I didn't do anything!" she replied, probably connecting the idea of happiness to the fact that she didn't

---

47. Rubin, *The Happiness Project.*

have a boyfriend, still had at least two years till graduation, and hadn't published any articles yet (which is important for doctoral students).

I was sad to hear her answer. She might have the mind-set that believes she has to reach success in order to be happy. That's sad, especially because sometimes it takes a long time to reach success, such as when we are doctoral students—it takes time to finish our coursework; it takes time to get approval to collect data; it takes time to conduct research; it takes time to write academic articles; it takes time to prepare a presentation; it takes time to write a dissertation, and so on. Even if doctoral students wait for small successes to happen during graduate school, it will take time to reach them. So why wait for something to happen to be happy? My friend's answer made feel grateful for realizing I didn't have to wait for big accomplishments to happen. I could be happy right there and then and, consequently, success would come.

Curious to know what friends who are not in the academic world would say, I texted a Brazilian friend: "What makes you happy?"

"What makes me happy??? What kind of question is that, Angelica???" he texted me back.

The reactions that I got from my friends about happiness surprised me because they didn't match people's natural desire to be happy. However, this made me realize that I had changed. If someone had asked me about happiness just a few months before, I would probably have reacted the same way they did. Not anymore. Reflecting on that, I realized I had gone beyond learning about happiness; I had *run into true happiness*! Nothing had changed about my academic semester. I was still taking three courses, teaching two undergraduate classes, tutoring several Japanese students, and driving back and forth between College Station and Houston. Yet, my life had changed. As a result of living mindfully and being aware of how I could bring happiness into my routine, I was feeling much happier. And best of all, my happiness was contagious.

One night, Kent unexpectedly said to me, "Honey, I really like that you are doing this happiness journey."

"Really? Why?" I asked curiously.

Using his hands as if they were the plates of a justice scale, he said, "Because *before*, your happiness level was down here. So your low happiness level dragged my happiness level from up here to down here." He placed his right hand, which showed his happiness level, slightly above his left hand, which indicated my happiness level. "But now, your high happiness level is up here, so mine is up here too, close to yours," he said as he showed his right hand (representing his happiness level) slightly below his left hand (representing my happiness level).

Noticing that his hands were not on the same level and knowing that he is constantly in a good mood, I asked, "Don't you mean that my high level of happiness brings your happiness to the same level as mine?"

"Nope! Your happiness journey has made you go beyond my happiness level. Nevertheless, your high level of happiness brings my happiness up."

That comment meant a lot to me, especially because it came from Kent, who was a role model of happiness. I remember my brother asking him one day, "Don't you ever get in a bad mood?"

Kent smiled and said, "Maybe sometimes when my football team loses." (Kent is a huge fan of the New England Patriots.)

I couldn't measure my happiness to compare *my old me* happiness level to the *new Angelica's* happiness level. But I could definitely feel I was a lot happier, and Kent's comments just confirmed that. I was not only happier but also making others happier.

I was grateful for all the new knowledge that I had learned from Vieira, Achor, Robbins, and Rubin. Their work led me into a path that in the beginning seemed like a maze because I wasn't sure exactly where it was going to take me, except for a life better than before. However, my dedication and commitment to what I learned from them guided me to the way out of the maze and showed me that was the path to *lasting happiness*—that is, *the practice of habits based on my principles and beliefs that match my own life expectations.*

If I wanted, I could have stopped my happiness journey at that point and simply continued putting into practice what I had already learned. But that was when I took Rubin's the *Four Tendencies* quiz and realized I wasn't an *Upholder*, as I believed I was. I am an *Obliger*. So I had more to learn. If you are not familiar with those tendencies terms, I will explain in chapter 5.

WHAT ABOUT YOU?

- *What commandments would you create for yourself?*
- *What are three resolutions that could bring more happiness into your everyday life?*
- *Who is your spiritual master? Why?*
- *Are you happy?*
- *What makes you happy?*

Five

CREATING HABITS

According to Rubin's research for her book *Better Than Before*, our expectations play a great role in our progress of creating new habits. She focused on two types of expectations: *outer* expectations (e.g., to meet deadlines) and *inner* expectations (e.g., to stop eating junk food). Based on how people react to those types of expectations, she created the *Four Tendencies*: *Upholder*, *Questioner*, *Obliger*, and *Rebel*. Below is a brief description of each tendency.[48]

Upholders: People who meet outer and inner expectations. They are highly disciplined people. They are very good at checking everything off their to-do lists without any supervision. They like rules and would feel uncomfortable even being with someone who is not following a rule, such as using a cell phone when not allowed.

Questioners: People who resist outer expectations but meet inner expectations. They like to question things they hear or read. They are willing to learn from experts on a particular topic, but they make decisions based on their own judgments and what is best for them.

---

48. Rubin, *Better Than Before*, Self-Knowledge, The Fateful Tendencies We Bring into the World section.

Obligers: People who meet outer expectations but resist inner expectations. They struggle to keep habits because they need external accountability. Also, they like to please others. So since it's hard for them to say no to other people, they end up neglecting their own priorities.

Rebels: People who resist outer and inner expectations. They do what *they* want to do. They don't like to follow rules or expectations dictated by others.

After learning about the Four Tendencies, I didn't even think of taking the quiz Rubin designed for people to identify their tendency. Seeing myself as a goal-oriented, disciplined, hardworking, and high-achieving person, I had no doubt I was an Upholder, until I was proven otherwise.

One day, I dropped off a friend at the airport and ended up being stuck there for hours. There was a thunderstorm in Houston, so I couldn't go back home because of a flood warning. And if you know Houston, you know that we shouldn't ignore flood warnings. While waiting for it to be safe to drive back home, I decided to take the Four Tendencies quiz.[49] To my astonishment, the results read: "According to your answers, your dominant Tendency is Obliger." Below is the brief description of Obligers that followed the results.

Obligers respond readily to outer expectations, but struggle to meet inner expectations. In other words, they work hard not to let other people down, but they often let themselves down.

Obligers may find it difficult to form a habit, because often we undertake habits for our own benefit, and Obligers do things more easily for others than for themselves.

For Obligers, the *key* to forming habits is to create *external accountability*.[50]

---

49. Rubin, "The Four Tendencies."
50. Ibid.

Obliger? What happened to me being an Upholder? I had even told Rubin I was an Upholder in my e-mail to her. After receiving the quiz results, I felt like I wasn't honest with her. But I am sure it wouldn't make any difference for her to know that a stranger was surprised to know she didn't have an Upholder tendency. Nevertheless, it made a difference to me. As a perfectionist and high-achieving person who doesn't like to depend on others to accomplish things, I wasn't satisfied with the quiz results suggesting that my strong tendency was Obliger.

The rain outside the airport was just getting stronger and stronger, so I had a lot of time to reflect on those results. As I tried to understand why my dominant tendency was Obliger, I resisted accepting it, despite the evidence of my Obliger characteristics. For example, in chapter 2, I described how challenging it was for me to say no because I didn't want to disappoint anyone. As a consequence, many times I said yes to other people's priorities while saying no to my own priorities. Although my new-me journey helped me be more assertive and attentive to my goals, the quiz results suggested there was still room for improvement in that area.

Here are three other signs of me being an Obliger. First, a few semesters ago, I created a writing group with other graduate students. Every meeting, I asked all the group members to create a writing goal for the following week and report writing accomplishments they had that current week. Despite the fact that the meetings could benefit everybody in the group, deep inside, I created the writing group to have an *external accountability* that would encourage *me* to create and achieve my writing goals because I knew I would have to report them to my colleagues.

The second sign of me being an Obliger was that I made a weekly appointment with a POWER consultant. Goodson, a professor at Texas A&M University, initiated the POWER (Promoting Outstanding Writing for Excellence in Research) services. The service is provided for Texas A&M University graduate students and faculty who want to improve writing skills or simply receive feedback on their writing. Throughout the whole academic year, at the beginning of each month, I went to the POWER website to make a weekly appointment with a consultant. That way I didn't even have to take time during the week to make the decision whether I should have a POWER appointment or not. Knowing myself, if I had already scheduled an appointment, I wouldn't miss it. I was grateful for the POWER service because it encouraged me to keep up with my writing, which not only improved my writing abilities but also helped me finish my papers a few days before the deadline. The POWER consultant served as an *external accountability* to "force" me to write regularly.

The other sign of being an Obliger was my weekly meetings with my friend Nasser, who was also pursuing his PhD. Unfortunately, he doesn't live in College Station anymore. I enjoyed having Nasser as a classmate and friend because he is a goal-oriented person like me. Besides, we share the same research interest, so we supported each other in our academic work. A few months after he left, I e-mailed him.

```
Hi Nasser,

I know that now we are busy with all the school-
work we have to do. But, if you agree, I'd love to
collaborate with you in future studies. I think
it would be great for us to work together be-
cause we have similar research interests. What
do you think?

Take care,
Angelica
```

Nasser replied to my e-mail on the following day.

Hi Angelica,

I am honestly eager to collaborate with you to publish some papers that cover our common interests. I know that you are hardworking, super organized and motivated. Furthermore, to get into academia both of us need to get some good papers published. So, please do not hesitate to let me know if I could be of any help in any project that is related to social media, virtual reality, massively multiplayer online games, e-learning or some topics like teacher education.

Wish you all the best,
Nasser

Soon after we exchanged those e-mails, Nasser and I started meeting on Skype every week. Our meetings have served different purposes. They allow us to maintain our friendship, support each other, exchange research ideas, and work together on projects. Since we started meeting regularly, we have collected data for some collaborative projects on teaching a second language, got a research proposal accepted at an international conference, and submitted a manuscript to a teacher education journal. Once again, by inviting Nasser to collaborate with me on projects and meet on a weekly basis to discuss research ideas, I not only wanted to work with him, but I was also looking for *external accountability* to be productive in my academic life.

After giving much thought to being an Obliger, I said to myself, "You know what? I don't want to be an Obliger. I want to be an Upholder because I don't want to rely on anything or anyone to be able to accomplish my goals, no matter if they are small or big goals. Since I am already a determined and disciplined person, it will be easy for me to become an Upholder. I just have to strengthen my habits and have better self-control."

It was important to me to become an Upholder because, in my view, Upholders are very productive, since they meet their outer and inner expectations. One of the findings of my happiness journey was that productivity made me very happy. Therefore, being an Upholder, I could be even happier in life.

My desire to be an Upholder led me to invest in my happiness journey even more. As an Obliger, I could already meet outer expectations, so to become an Upholder, all I needed to do was be able to meet (as opposed to resist) inner expectations. To meet inner expectations, I would have to use my assertive skills; increase my self-control and discipline; and learn more about happiness, habits, time management, and productivity. With that said, here are some actions I took in an attempt to change my tendency. I volunteered as a "Super Fan" on Rubin's website to be updated with her work, receive book recommendations, and get a "moment of happiness quote." Also, having in mind the importance of journaling about a positive experience, I bought Rubin's journal called *The Happiness Project: One Sentence Journal* to encourage me to write, even if it was only one sentence long. Additionally, based on Achor's notion that happiness leads us to success, I started using the Happify app, which is designed to boost people's happiness through different activities, such as the Negative Knockout game. Moreover, I started wearing colorful bands tied to my watch to remind me of my happiness journey. I organized all my little sources of happiness (e.g., circle-of-life goals, gratitudes, acts of kindness, my commandments, and resolutions) in what I titled My Happiness Habit Journal (which is described in chapter 7). Furthermore, I bought more books and audiobooks and listened to more lectures on happiness, habits, time management, productivity, confidence, and even on the power of the mind. As a result, before the end of the semester, I had already incorporated three new daily routines, which were added to My Happiness Habit Journal. The new routines were the implementation of tiny habits, meditation, and happy moments.

Tiny Habits

In a TED Talk, B. J. Fogg, a professor from Stanford University, encouraged the implementation of tiny habits (e.g., floss one tooth at a time) in order to acquire a bigger habit (e.g., floss all our teeth every day). He explained the effectiveness of tiny habits by saying that if we want to make a long-term change by creating a new habit, we need to make sure the new behavior is systematic and automatic. In other words, no decisions are necessary to perform the new habit. Therefore, practice and repetitions are essential for new behavior to become automatic. By breaking down a new habit, we are then providing practice of the new behavior we want to incorporate in our lives. Additionally, by breaking down a new habit, we are making it easier to be performed, and as a result, it increases our motivation to do it.[51]

As Fogg noted, for a tiny habit to be effective, we need to consider three important elements: motivation, ability, and trigger. Besides having some motivation to do the tiny habit, we need to have the ability to perform it and have a trigger to remind us to do the tiny habit. The trigger is essential because without it, we will most likely forget to perform the tiny habit. A great way to trigger the new behavior (i.e., the tiny habit) is to tie it to a behavior you already have. Fogg suggested the following formula to help us tie a new behavior to an old one: *after I* (a behavior I already have), *I will* (the new behavior I want to create).[52]

51. Fogg, "Start With a Tiny Habit."
52. Ibid.

For example, if I already exercise regularly and want to create the habit of drinking more water, I can say, *After I exercise, I will drink a glass of water.*

Fogg's idea of tiny habits seemed very easy to implement. But my goals were to keep improving my assertiveness, confidence, happiness, and productivity. Would tiny habits work for my big abstract goals? The only way to find out was to give the formula a try. So I did.

Because I wanted to make sure to master each tiny habit, I created just a few every month and then carried them out the following month and so on. Here are five tiny habits I created.

After I Start Walking, I Will Look Up

As a result of my new-me journey or my happiness journey, my assertiveness and confidence had already improved a great deal, but I wanted to improve them even more because they would positively impact my happiness, productivity, and consequently my success. So the question was "What tiny habits can lead me to assertiveness and confidence?" The answer came from the books *The Six Pillars of Self-Esteem* by Nathaniel Branden and *Choose the Life You Want* by Ben-Shahar. According to them, body language and affirmations can improve assertiveness and confidence.

Ben-Shahar stated that "the way we hold our bodies sends the message not only to others, but also to ourselves."[53] For example, when we walk with our heads down and drag our feet, we show lack of energy and confidence. On the other hand, when we walk with our heads up, sit straight, and shake hands firmly, for instance, we transmit confidence, motivation, and energy not only to those around us but to ourselves—even if we don't feel confident or energetic.[54] That goes to show

---

53. Ben-Shahar, *Choose the Life You Want*, Choice 5.
54. Ibid.

that our behavior impacts how we feel. If we want to change how we feel, we have to change how we behave.

Keeping this in mind, my first tiny habit was *after I start walking, I will look up.* This tiny habit might seem meaningless to people who are already confident. But it was very meaningful to me because it wasn't a habit for me to look up (which gave me the advantage of protecting myself from falling or tripping). Knowing that I could improve my assertiveness just by looking up seemed easy and worth it. I simply needed to create the habit of keeping my head up while walking. It took me a while to get used to looking up, but the trigger (i.e., to start walking) helped me create the new behavior. With time, just looking up gave me the "sense of having the right to belong to the world as much as anyone else," as Branden pointed out as an important factor of self-esteem.[55] As a result, I increased my self-respect and self-esteem.

AFTER I TOUCH MY FACE, I WILL SAY, "I AM ASSERTIVE AND CONFIDENT"
Ben-Shahar explained the importance of affirmations based on the notion of self-concept, which affects our thoughts and behavior. Our self-concept, how we see ourselves, can be positive or negative.[56] For example, one of my self-concepts was that I wasn't confident. The good news is that we can change our self-concept. One way to do that is by combining our thoughts with our behavior through the repetition of affirmations or sentences positively stating what we want to see in ourselves.[57] Since repetition and persistence are essential in this exercise, I created my second tiny habit: *after I touch my face, I will say, "I am assertive and confident."* I don't know about you, but I often touch my face. So I was reminded several times throughout the day that I am assertive and confident. As Ben-Shahar said, when we plant new positive

---

55. Branden, *The Six Pillars of Self-Esteem.*
56. Ben-Shahar, *Choose the Life You Want,* Choice 67.
57. Ibid.

messages, negative messages eventually "lose their centrality and their overwhelming power and have less influence on us."[58] My experience with this tiny habit showed that affirming positive messages can be a powerful way to change our self-concept.

After I Meditate, I Will Text Three Friends or Family Members
Then, the question became, "What tiny habits can lead me to more happiness, which, consequently, will help me be more successful?" The answer to that question surprised me. Supported by several happiness experts, psychiatrist and Harvard professor Robert Waldinger reported that social connections are the best predictor of happiness. In his TED Talk ("What Makes a Good Life?"), Waldinger shared lessons from the longest study on happiness. The study's findings contradicted the idea that happiness can mainly come from money, fame, or work.

For seventy-five years, researchers from Harvard University followed the lives of 724 men, who were college students at the beginning of the study. Using multiple sources of data, ranging from observing participants at work and home to scanning their brains and drawing their blood, researchers found that good relationships are what keep us healthier and happier. Social connections make people stay healthier, feel happier, and have longer lives. However, it is worth mentioning that what matters in social connections is not the number of friends or family members we have, but the *quality* of our relationships. People who have good relationships are physically and mentally happier and healthier. Therefore, the findings of that study suggest we should build and maintain strong relationships, spend more quality time with people, and forgive others.[59]

The fact that the best predictor of happiness is social connections reinforced the importance of the *social* and *family* components from the

---

58. Ibid.
59. Waldinger, "What Makes a Good Life?"

circle of life. In chapter 1, I mentioned that I created a small concrete goal for each circle-of-life component for me to address every day. My goal for the social and family components was to keep in touch with my friends and family. To make sure my busy schedule didn't stop me from achieving that daily goal, I started the following tiny habit: *after I meditate, I will text three friends or family members.* Such a tiny habit might seem meaningless for some people, but it was very meaningful to me. As a PhD student, I had already experienced the stressful and lonely life that students might have as a result of graduate schoolwork (if they don't do anything to avoid such a life). Creating that tiny habit ensured I made time for social connections.

You may have noticed that I attached that tiny habit to meditation—something that, as mentioned in chapter 2, I had failed to implement in my everyday routine. Later in this chapter, I will explain how I turned meditation into a habit.

After I Touch My Hair, I Will Smile

Another tiny habit to lead me to more happiness involved smiling, a way our bodies use to express our feelings. Ben-Shahar expanded on the idea that what we do with our bodies reflects our thoughts and feelings by explaining the facial feedback hypothesis.[60] That hypothesis states that our facial expressions dictate how we feel. So a smile will lead us to more positive feelings, as opposed to a frown, which will lead us to more negative feelings. Therefore, if we want to improve our mood, we should smile or laugh, even if we have to fake it. As Achor explained, we have mirror neurons, which "are receptors in our brains that cause us to unconsciously mimic the actions of those around us. When we see someone perform an action, like a yawn or a smile, our mirror neurons light up and signal our bodies to perform that same motion."[61]

---

60. Ben-Shahar, *Choose the Life You Want*, Choice 39.
61. Achor, *Before Happiness*, Skill 5, The Five-Star Hospital Contagious Realities section.

That means that when we smile because we saw someone smiling, our brains believe that we are going through a positive situation. Our smiles, then, make our brains release chemicals such as dopamine. The released chemicals reduce negative feelings, improve our mood, make us feel happier, and help us see positive realities.[62]

The benefits of a smile could certainly help me with my goal of being more productive and happier. By seeing positive realities, it would be easier for me to find solutions to problems, make me interpret difficult situations as challenges as opposed to threats, make the environment more pleasurable, and bring me more positive feelings. All that would help me be more productive at work and happier in life. So what tiny habit could I create to encourage me to smile more? After thinking for a while, I finally came up with a perfect tiny habit for me. Knowing that I often touch my hair (like many other women), I created the following tiny habit: *after I touch my hair, I will smile.*

One day, when I shared with my cousin Jane how effective that tiny habit was, she asked, "So every time you touch your hair, you laugh?"

"No, I don't *laugh*. I simply smile. People might think that I am crazy if I suddenly laugh out of the blue," I answered as I imagined myself walking around the Texas A&M University campus, attending or teaching my classes, or working out at the gym and suddenly laughing out loud every time I touched my hair.

My new habit of smiling every time I touched my hair became so automatic that one day I caught myself doing it when there was no room for smiles. I was in my philosophy class. We were a class with only eight students, so we used a small classroom, where we all sat around a rectangular table to easily see everybody's faces. The professor was telling a sad story of someone who had passed away when I decided to—yes, touch my hair, which automatically—yes, made me smile. Fortunately, I quickly realized it and bent my head so nobody would see me smiling.

---

62. Ibid.

I mention this story to illustrate how powerful tiny habits can be if we take them seriously. They can definitely make changes in our lives.

Meditation

Speaking of changes, I decided to include one more habit in my life: meditation. After watching Achor's TED Talk, "The Happy Secret to Better Work," I tried to meditate because meditation was one of the suggested activities for creating lasting positive change for our brains to work more successfully. Since I couldn't stop my mind, not even for two minutes, I had given up on the idea of meditating. However, I decided to give meditation a second chance.

Lyubomirsky, a professor of psychology at the University of California, Riverside, said that we should choose strategies and activities that might bring us happiness based on our personalities and ways of life.[63] Although I could have used her advice as an excuse not to practice meditation, I couldn't overlook all the benefits either. The more I learned about happiness, the more I became aware of the importance of meditation. The numerous benefits of meditation are well summarized in Lyubomirsky's book *The How of Happiness*. In her own words, meditation is a powerful activity that can

- boost both physical and psychological well-being;
- produce true happiness by realizing a state of awareness and detachment;
- affect your brain activity and your immune system;
- be effective in patients with heart disease, chronic pain, skin disorders, and a variety of mental health conditions such as depression, anxiety, panic, and substance abuse;

---

63. Lyubomirsky, *The How of Happiness*.

- help people who are ill (and everyone else, for that matter) because it reduces their reactivity to stress and boosts positive mood, self-esteem, and feelings of control; and
- benefit such seemingly intractable characteristics as intelligence, creativity, and cognitive flexibility in the elderly.[64]

Faced with so many potential benefits that meditation can bring to our lives, I couldn't ignore it anymore. So one day in December, about three months after I had given up meditation, I said to Kent, "I've decided to include the habit of meditation in my daily routine. Even if I don't notice any direct benefits from it, I'm sure it will help me somehow because I have never heard any argument against meditation. On the contrary, I only hear arguments in its favor." With that said, based on Fogg's ideas on how to start a new habit, I created the following tiny habit: *after I exercise, I will meditate for five minutes.*

As I looked for a very simple way to meditate, I chose to adapt a relaxation exercise that psychologist Neil Fiore mentioned in his book *The Now Habit.* He recommended a relaxation exercise as a technique to overcome procrastination and instead create a positive mind-set for us to move on to our everyday activities. According to Fiore, during the relaxation exercise, we should focus our attention on our breathing as we let go of the past and future and then center our minds in the present. I adapted his technique to keep it simple. I simply took a deep breath, held it for a moment, and exhaled slowly while saying to myself, "My mind is clear." Then, again, I took a deep breath, held it for a moment, and exhaled slowly while saying to myself, "My body is relaxed." I repeated the same procedure for five minutes. After getting used to that routine, I was amazed to notice that I did clear my mind and felt my body was relaxed by simply stating "My mind is clear" and "My body is relaxed," as I focused on my breathing. As Fiore said, by

---

64. Ibid., Chapter 9, Happiness Activity No. 12, Why Meditate? section.

allowing my body to relax, my subconscious mind helped me achieve a deeper relaxation process.[65]

I was happy to have given meditation a second chance. I did notice its immediate benefits—after meditating, I felt like I had pressed a reset button on my mind and body. Even knowing I had a busy schedule ahead, my five-minute meditation made me feel good, calm, positive, and ready to have a productive day and to face whatever challenges it could bring.

Happy Moments

Still trying to become an Upholder (i.e., someone who can meet inner and outer expectations) as a way to be more productive and therefore happier, I started to take notes of two happy moments I had every day. My happy moment list was based on the boosting-our-happiness exercise proposed by Ben-Shahar in his book *Happier*. He said that we should create a list of activities that are meaningful and pleasurable to us. Those activities, called *happiness boosters*, provide us with present and future benefits as well as transform our states.[66] For example, happiness boosters can change an uninspiring to an inspiring state, a tiring to an invigorating state, an unmotivated to a motivated state, and a dull to an energetic state. It is important that we are aware of our happiness boosters so that we make use of them, especially when we want to improve our states. Examples of my happiness boosters or happy moments are taking a break from my studies to get a cup of coffee with a friend, talking to Kent or watching a sitcom with him, and watching a video about happiness.

The simple fact that by nighttime I would have to identify two happy moments that happened throughout my day encouraged me to look forward to experiencing happiness boosters. As a result, I was happier

---

65. Fiore, *The Now Habit*, Chapter 7, Relaxation Exercise section.
66. Ben-Shahar, *Happier*, Chapter 10.

and more energetic during the day. Moreover, the habit of identifying happy moments served as a reminder that it was up to me to improve my state if needed.

End-of-Semester Self-Reflection

When the fall semester was over, Kent and I went to spend the holidays with his relatives in Michigan. While we were there, I took some time to reflect on my happiness journey. Although I incorporated new habits to improve my assertive skills, self-control, discipline, and productivity as an attempt to be an Upholder, I wasn't sure if I could really change my Obliger tendency. Nevertheless, while reflecting on my fall semester, I was amazed to realize how much I had accomplished within only four months. I'm sure it was because I was living a more mindful life. Looking back, I was astonished to see that in the beginning of the semester, it was a struggle to figure out how I was going to find time to do everything I had committed to. I had to complete all the requirements of the three courses I was going to take, teach two undergraduate classes, and tutor several Japanese students—all that as I drove back and forth from Houston to College Station. However, at the end of the semester, I had not only succeeded in my graduate courses and teaching assignments, but I was also able to accomplish things that I had not even planned.

On top of my busy schedule that semester, I still had time to spend with three relatives who visited with me and Kent for about a week (each of whom came at a different time). On Thanksgiving Day, besides having friends over for dinner, Kent and I volunteered for Operation Turkey, an organization that delivers more than forty thousand meals to the homeless and less fortunate. I also went through all my clothes and donated several bags of unused items. Rubin inspired me to go through my closet and get rid of clothes that I didn't use anymore.[67] Since I

---

67. Rubin, *The Happiness Project.*

didn't have much "free" time, every day throughout the semester, I put one piece of clothing in the donation pile. By the end of the semester, I had donated several bags. My action ended up inspiring Kent. One day he said, "Are you ready for this?"

"For what?" I asked.

"I want you to choose twenty of my shirts to donate."

"Really?" I was amazed to see how much he trusted my taste! As I went through his drawers, I thought, *This is my chance to get rid of that green shirt*, a shirt that for some reason I didn't like on him. In the end, with my help, Kent ended up donating two full bags of clothes.

By the end of fall, I also finally finished reading the book *Someday, Someday, Maybe* by Lauren Graham. (I am a big fan of her work, especially in *Gilmore Girls* and *Parenthood*.) I had been trying to finish that book for a while. Another accomplishment was to organize the coupon bag, which I had meant to do for at least a year. Unfortunately, most of the coupons had already expired, but I was happy simply to finally go through them! As for my academic life, by the end of the semester, I had received approval from the university to conduct a research project and submitted a manuscript to an education journal.

As a result of everything I experienced through my new-me journey or my happiness journey, I had lived a meaningful, productive, and most importantly, happy semester in all areas of my life: *health, social, relationship with a significant other, family, spiritual, emotional, professional, financial, intellectual,* and *service.*

I didn't have any measuring tool to prove that my new habits and mind-set improved my self-esteem, assertiveness, mood, work performance, social connections, and relationships, which altogether resulted in a happier life. However, I was sure that my happiness was a result of my new habits and mind-set because nothing new had happened in my life. I hadn't graduated, gotten a new job, received a raise, had children, moved to a new house, or bought a car. At the end of the semester, I was still a graduate student, working hard to become a professor. The difference was that I had learned the habits and ways of thinking that could lead me to the path of my long-lasting happiness.

BEING HUMAN

It is important to mention that while living a happier life, I wasn't happy all the time. There were times when I felt upset and sad. Here's one of the few moments when I didn't feel happy during that fall semester. As Rubin warned *The Happiness Project* readers, the call—the one that will upend your entire progress—does come. After receiving a call in mid-December, I felt very angry and sad about some family issues. Before receiving the call, I was sitting at my computer, totally focused on my work. I was filling out an IRB (Institutional Review Board) form through the university to obtain approval to conduct a study. Then, I was going to grade my undergraduate students' assignments. However, soon after I sat down to work on the IRB form, I got the call, which completely took me out of my let's-be-productive state. That call led to other calls that just made me even sadder and more upset. When I hung up, I put my head down and cried, but within thirty seconds, I tried to control my emotions.

"What happened to my happiness journey? I should be happy and not sad or angry," I said to myself. But I had no strength to put a smile on my face (not even if I touched my hair) or even to bring a happy thought to my mind. Then I thought, *I should just allow myself to be sad, to feel angry. I spent the last six months working on my happiness journey. I was so careful to control my negative thoughts and feelings.* Remembering Ben-Shahar's words, I told myself, "So it's OK, Angelica. It's OK to be human." In his book *Choose the Life You Want*, he said that we should allow ourselves to be human because painful emotions are part of life, and if we force ourselves not to experience them, they just become more intense and will negatively affect us even more. I then decided to allow myself to be sad.

Whenever I am sad, I like to talk to someone who really loves and cares about me. So I went to the living room to talk to Kent. I lay down next to him and cried. I was still deeply sad but happy to have a very supportive husband who is always there for me. My feelings didn't change after talking to Kent, but his support, together with my decision to allow myself to be human (as opposed to ignoring those negative feelings and just storing them inside of me), made me stronger.

It was already ten o'clock at night, and the IRB form and my students' assignments were still waiting for me. Although they were not due that day, I knew that getting this work done would make me feel better because it would give me the feeling of productivity and accomplishment. So I took the time to get it done that same night. But first, I remembered the importance of exercise from the book *The Happiness Advantage* by Achor. He said that exercise is a powerful tool for several reasons, one of them being that the effects of exercise are equivalent to an antidepressant medication. They are actually better because the effects of exercise last longer than antidepressants. With that in mind, I exercised to feel more energetic and to bring some happiness hormones, such as endorphins, into my body. That night I went to bed at three o'clock after submitting the IRB form and grading all my students' assignments. It was a rough evening, but it ended well because of the decisions I made: be human, look for support, and do something that would make me feel better. Without my happiness journey, I don't think I would have made those decisions. As Kent said to me, "Your happiness journey should not be about making you happy all the time but helping you handle difficult situations."

Happiness Indicators

Although I experienced sad moments throughout the semester, they were very rare. I was certainly happy most of the time. As Daniel Gilbert pointed out in his book *Stumbling on Happiness*, there is no *happyometer*, a reliable instrument to accurately measure our happiness level. *We* are the best observers of our feelings; therefore, the best way to evaluate our happiness is through our own observations of our feelings. Having said that, I could simply say that I was feeling happier than before and hope that you believed me. However, in addition to simply saying that I was truly happier at the end of the fall semester, I would like to share three major signs that served as indicators of my happiness improvement.

My first happiness indicator was my lack of cold sores on my mouth. Since I was a teenager, I have had cold sores on my mouth several times a year. Although cold sores can be caused by things like shared eating utensils or a kiss by someone with a cold sore, those were never the causes of *my* cold sores as long as I can remember. Instead, whenever I felt very sad or upset or experienced situations in which I reacted with stress, anxiety, fear, or great discomfort, I was stamped with a cold sore right on the outside of my mouth. Unfortunately, my lack of assertiveness or confidence didn't prevent me from having cold sores. On the contrary, they encouraged cold-sore outbreaks. Although there is no cure for cold sores, when I was sixteen years old, getting ready to come to the United States as an exchange student, I was advised to take a vaccine that would prevent me from having cold sores for about one year. My parents and I agreed that the vaccine would be a good idea so that I wouldn't have to worry about cold-sore outbreaks while living one year abroad. So I took the vaccine for several months in order to be cold sore free by the time I had to leave Brazil. The thought of not having cold sores for about one whole year was such a relief for me.

The week before flying to Massachusetts was very busy with good-bye parties, packing, and trips to stores. At the good-bye parties, I heard the following statements from several people: "You are so brave to go away for a whole year. I could never do that!" "Aren't you afraid of going to a place where you are not proficient in their language?" "Doesn't it make you nervous to go live with a family who you never saw before?" "I bet you will miss your family a lot!" As I heard all that, I did my best to only stick with the "You are so brave" statement. Throughout the months leading up to the trip to the United States, I was tempted to rethink my plan to participate in the exchange-program experience. However, I ignored all the discouraging thoughts that came to my mind because deep inside I knew that if I stopped to carefully think about everything I was about to face, I wouldn't leave my hometown, family, friends, culture, or comfort of my home. It was 1994. I was only sixteen years old; I didn't know much English; I didn't know my host family; I had never left Brazil; and I didn't have a cell phone (cell phones weren't mainstream at the time) or Internet to keep in touch with my family and friends. Yet I ignored all that and came to this country.

Although I did my very best to overlook my discouraging thoughts before leaving my hometown, my body couldn't ignore them. To my surprise, although I thought my mind and body could be tricked, I noticed a cold sore on my mouth as I said good-bye to my family at the airport in Fortaleza. That cold-sore experience showed me that my anxiety and emotional stress were stronger than a vaccine. That experience also scared me because I realized that I didn't really know how to control my feelings. What scared me the most was that I was already walking away from my family and toward the plane as I was having that realization. Needless to say, I had many other cold-sore outbreaks throughout my exchange-program year and all the following years of my life; they were all due to negative emotional feelings.

Fast-forward to 2015, and until the spring semester of that year, cold sores were still part of my life. I was so used to them that it was very easy to predict when I was going to have one. However, since I started my new-me journey, I haven't had any cold-sore outbreaks! My new cold-sore-free life may not seem like a big deal for many people (especially those who haven't experienced them) because it is not linked to their well-being. Nevertheless, it means a lot to me! Being free from cold sores doesn't only mean I am happy for not having to go through feeling embarrassed or uncomfortable for several days because of them. My lack of cold sores also means I have learned to control my anxiety, stress, frustration, and any other negative feelings that were affecting my immune system. Most importantly, it means that I have learned how to create happiness in my everyday life.

My second major happiness indicator was deciding to quit my appointments with Dr. Sarah, my therapist. Every time we had an appointment scheduled, I would take some minutes to jot down issues I wanted to share. Again, back then, my lack of confidence and assertiveness made it very easy for me to create an unpleasant-experience list to discuss with her.

Despite really enjoying talking with Dr. Sarah and being very grateful for all the patience, attention, and knowledge she shared with me, toward the end of the fall semester, I started noticing that my conversation topics with her were changing from negative to positive. We used to spend the entire appointments discussing only issues that bothered me. However, since I started my new-me journey, I noticed that the appointments were gradually becoming more and more about everything I was learning in terms of having a successful and happy life, as well as all the realizations and accomplishments that I was experiencing every day. It finally came to a point that I was having a very hard time coming up with problems to discuss with her. So I thought, *Well, if I have to think very hard to try to come up with something that is bothering me, it means that nothing is really bothering me. If I really had any issues, I wouldn't even have to try to remember what they are.* And that was true. There were times when I said to Dr. Sarah, "I couldn't think of any issues to discuss with you today, but let me tell you some great things that have happened to me and what I have learned about." I would share something I learned from researchers and experts on happiness. One day I even told her, "I must be your favorite patient because I come here just to tell you good things that have happened to me." That was when

I realized I didn't need a therapist anymore. I was truly grateful for Dr. Sarah's support and for witnessing the process from *my old me* to *my new me*. But it was time for me to move on and take full responsibility for my own happiness.

Finally, my third main indicator of happiness was making the decision to write this book. In December, while I spent an afternoon with my friend Mary, I said to her, "Mary, I've decided to write a book."

"Really? What is it going to be about?" she asked.

"It's going to be about happiness. You know, many successful people, such as book writers, actors, and actresses, were ordinary people just like me and you before they became famous. I'm sure they achieved great accomplishments due to their hard work and dedication. So if they could do something challenging like writing a book or playing a role in a movie, I can do it too. Well, I'm not sure about being an actress, but I can write a book."

"Definitely! I totally agree. Anyone can achieve whatever they set as goals. They only need to be persistent and work hard," Mary agreed with me.

"Exactly. And I am a very determined person, so I know I can write a book. I just need the time to write it. Since winter break is coming up, I decided to start it as soon as the academic semester is over."

"Wow, look at you, all confident!"

Similar to Dr. Sarah, Mary also witnessed the process I went through from *my old me* to *my new me*. She is such a good friend who has always been there to support me and applaud my accomplishments. As I started gradually becoming more assertive and confident in how I reacted to situations, Mary would jokingly say, with a surprised look, "Who is *that* person? I don't recognize *that* Angelica!"

I would smile and reply, "Well, start getting used to this new Angelica."

Going back to the book idea, I said to Mary, "Remember that I have been putting into practice all those extraordinary life strategies, brain exercises, tiny habits, resolutions, my commandments, and so on to have a more successful and happier life?"

"Yes," she answered attentively.

"Mary, they really work!"

"I know! I don't even recognize you anymore. Where is that afraid, insecure, and unassertive Angelica?"

"She's gone," I said, laughing. "So I want to share with other people everything I went through because if I could change through my new-me journey or my happiness journey, I believe other people can too."

"Well, I'm very proud of you, and I'm here to support you," Mary said.

"Good to know, because I was wondering if you could read the draft of the book and give me feedback on it?" I asked her. Mary was very sincere and meticulous, so she was an excellent person to give me feedback.

"Absolutely!"

Mary's support just reinforced my determination to start writing this book. By the time I came back from the holidays in Michigan, I already had the draft of the first two chapters ready for Mary to read. I couldn't wait to get her feedback! Everything I wrote was interesting and made sense to me. But would readers find it interesting too? Would it make sense for them? Most importantly, would it positively impact their lives?

A few weeks later, Mary shared with me what she thought of the book's draft. She said, "I enjoyed reading the draft of your book! It was very inspiring and very encouraging. It inspired me to change things about me and how I view things. It actually made me want to try some strategies for myself, especially the ones related to self-improvement and self-motivation. After putting them into practice, my mood changed drastically. I feel myself being happier, and my coworkers have even noticed it."

"Amazing, Mary, especially because I have not even written the chapter on happiness yet," I said.

I was speechless with Mary's feedback. I wasn't just happy that she enjoyed the draft of my book, but mainly that the ideas included in my book had positively impacted her own life.

I was so energized to continue my commitment to writing this book. It was clear that I was living a much happier life; I wouldn't have been able to spread happiness if I weren't happy myself.

WHAT ABOUT YOU?

- *Which one is your tendency: Upholder, Questioner, Obliger, or Rebel? Take Gretchen Rubin's Four Tendencies quiz to find out. You can find the quiz at this website: http://www.surveygizmo.com/s3/3163256/ Gretchen-Rubin-s-Quiz-The-Four-Tendencies-Fall2016.*
- *I created my tiny habits based on what I wanted to improve in my life, such as my confidence and happiness. What are two things you would like to improve in your life? What tiny habits can you create to help improve those two things?*
- *Have you ever meditated? If yes, how did it help you? If no, would you consider adding meditation to your routine so that you can bring its benefits into your life?*
- *What are two happy moments you had today?*
- *Describe a difficult situation when you felt better by allowing yourself to be human.*
- *The lack of cold-sore outbreaks was one of my happiness indicators. What are some of your happiness indicators?*

Six

Sharing New Lessons to a Happier Life

Spring 2016 came. It was a busy semester, but not as busy as the previous semester. In the spring, I took a second statistics course, which was taught by the same professor I had in the fall, Dr. James. That meant that once again I would spend a great deal of time studying statistics by reading the textbook, completing the course assignments, attending his classes, listening and taking notes on his lectures, and joining study-group meetings. Besides statistics, I took six credits of research, collected data for a study, and participated in a research group. My graduate assistantship assignment was to teach an undergraduate course and assist a professor with her course grading. With all I had to do on campus, I spent most of the week in College Station. I left Houston on Sundays and went back home on Thursdays. On Fridays, I spent the day tutoring Japanese students. Unfortunately, I spent most of the semester away from Kent.

During the spring, I kept learning about how to live a happier life while continuing to put into practice everything I had already learned the semester before (e.g., strategies for an extraordinary life, brain exercises, tiny habits, resolutions, and my commandments). In this chapter,

I share the following ten ideas that led me to an even happier life: (1) *finding sources of happiness,* (2) *making something meaningful,* (3) *controlling anxiety,* (4) *spreading the word,* (5) *using money for a happy purpose,* (6) *saving mental energy,* (7) *choosing happiness burgers,* (8) *choosing positive thoughts and words,* (9) *accepting ourselves,* and (10) *forgiving others.* For each idea, I explain its connection to happiness and provide one or more examples of situations when I implemented them during my spring semester.

Finding Sources of Happiness

In his book *Happier,* Ben-Shahar revealed four main sources of happiness. Happiness can come from something *meaningful, pleasurable, unpleasurable,* and *challenging.* After learning about the sources of happiness, I decided to incorporate them in my routine. Since then, I start the day identifying four sources of happiness—one for each category. However, some of the sources might overlap. For example, having a conversation with my grandma is a *meaningful* and *pleasurable* source of happiness. Unlike *meaningful* and *pleasurable* sources of happiness, *unpleasurable* and *challenging* ones may not immediately bring me happy feelings, but they certainly bring me good feelings later. Identifying sources of happiness makes me start my day looking forward to experiencing actions that will make me happier.

I have noticed that looking for sources of happiness has helped me in two ways. First, it changes my perspective on certain activities, especially unpleasant and challenging ones. For example, cleaning the house is an unpleasant task to me. I don't enjoy cleaning the house, but that activity brings me happiness after I complete it. So in this case, instead of seeing the activity of cleaning the house as a burden or something simply unpleasant, I see it as a source of happiness.

Another example of a source of happiness is my dissertation work. Working on my dissertation is challenging. However, I know that everything I do toward completing it brings me happiness. Therefore, instead of feeling overwhelmed with the amount of reading and writing I have to do to graduate, I focus on the fact that all I have to read and write is a source of happiness.

As Ben-Shahar said, not everything we do brings us present benefits. Sometimes it brings future benefits.[68] Based on my own experience, by keeping Ben-Shahar's words in mind, we can change the way we perceive situations and activities. Although certain situations and activities are unpleasant and challenging, our focus should be on the fact that they will make us feel happier in the future.

The second way that looking for sources of happiness has helped me is to be more understanding toward others, especially when their happiness is involved. Knowing that happiness can come from something *meaningful*, *pleasurable*, *unpleasurable*, and *challenging* explains why people find happiness in different situations and activities. For example, playing soccer makes *Kent* happy because it's something pleasurable for him; whereas, playing soccer doesn't make *me* happy. So knowing that soccer brings *him* happiness, I better understand and respect all the time and effort he puts into soccer.

Here is another example to show that knowing that people find happiness in different situations and activities helped me be more understanding. Early in the spring semester, my adviser told me that she was moving to another campus (out of the United States) because she was promoted. After first hearing the news, I had the impression I was just dreaming and soon the alarm was going to make me realize it was a dream. The alarm never went off. It was real.

"But don't worry. I will continue working with you through Skype and e-mails. However, if you want to have a new adviser, it is fine," she said.

---

68. Ben-Shahar, *Happier*, Chapter 2, The Happiness Archetype section.

"No, I definitely don't want to change my adviser, because I enjoy working with you, and besides, you are the expert on the topic I chose for my dissertation," I replied.

As we talked about how we were going to make the end of my doctoral program work, I kept thinking, *How can she leave College Station, having several doctoral advisees? It is her job to be here for us, especially at a university that has high expectations from doctoral students.* Then I looked carefully at her and noticed she looked happy as she shared her news. Noticing her happiness and reminding myself of the four sources of happiness that are unique for each person, I realized that instead of focusing on how I was going to accomplish the remaining requirements for the doctoral program, I should actually be happy for her. She had just received a promotion and was going to live closer to her family. I knew that she loved to work and be with her family. The same way I was taking action to feel happier, so was she. That mind-set made me immediately change the direction of the conversation.

"I will definitely miss seeing you around campus and working with you face-to-face, but I am very happy for you," I told her. "I know that this new position means a lot to you and that you will feel so much happier being closer to your family."

She smiled, agreeing with me. I continued, "And I feel grateful for having already taken all the doctoral-level courses that you taught."

She nodded with a smile.

"I know that Skype does work in terms of getting academic work done," I said. "I've been meeting with Nasser every week to discuss research projects, and it has worked well."

"Yes, it does work. I have already spent a few years working from another campus, and while I was there, I worked with seven doctoral students from this campus. They all graduated just fine, and I even published articles with them during that time."

A few minutes later, I left her office, sad to know that she was about to leave the United States but happy to know that her actions were making her happier. My happiness journey had taught me to find and appreciate happiness in others.

Making Something Meaningful

In his book *Before Happiness*, Achor pointed out that we should find meaning in what we do in our personal and professional lives. According to him, by making our tasks meaningful, we reduce our stress and anxiety as we create a positive reality. As a result of establishing a positive reality, we become more motivated, creative, energetic, and productive. Moreover, we become better problem solvers and achieve better results.

With that in mind, I decided to put into practice the ideas I learned from Achor on how to make tasks meaningful. An example of how I put his ideas into practice comes from the philosophy course I took in the fall of 2015. I have to admit that philosophy wasn't my favorite course; studying it felt like a burden sometimes. Since all my classmates showed great interest in philosophy, they inspired me to try to make it more meaningful. So I asked myself, "How can I find meaning in philosophy?" As I attempted to answer that question and find some concrete application of philosophy in my life, I asked my professor during the following class, "In practical terms, how can we use philosophy in our lives?"

"We can use philosophy in everything in our lives. For example, it can help us solve problems and analyze situations," my professor excitedly answered, implying that philosophy can contribute to our happiness. And he was right.

As I kept reading and listening to books on happiness, philosophers were often cited. For example, in her book *The Gratitude Diaries*, Janice Kaplan referred to the Greek philosopher Epictetus when arguing that we couldn't control everything that happened to us. As she paraphrased his words, she wrote, Epictetus "explained that a key to living right is understanding that we have power only over ourselves and our own reactions."[69]

Another example comes from Brian Tracy's book *No Excuses!* He stated, "Aristotle wrote that the ultimate aim of human life is to be happy. He said that the great question each of us must answer is '*How shall we live in order to be happy?*'"[70] It then became clear to me that philosophy was closely related to happiness.

Learning about the connection between philosophy and happiness was definitely helping me find meaning in my philosophy course. Additionally, my weekly FaceTime calls with Uncle Fontenele and Aunt Margareth made me find meaning in philosophy. They both enjoyed talking about philosophers, so every week they asked me what I had learned from my philosophy classes. Their interest in that subject motivated me to be meaningfully engaged in all my course tasks. As a result, I felt excited to share something new every week, which made the course content much easier to understand.

I noticed the course content was becoming easier while reading a philosophy book I borrowed from my colleague Mathew. Right after the very first philosophy class, I scanned the book and said to him, "It seems that the language of this book is very difficult to understand!"

"Really?" he said, as he gave me a look that seemed to disagree with what I had just said. But he didn't argue with me, probably because I am not a native English speaker like he is.

At the end of the semester, I went to his office to return the book. "Mathew, here's your book. Thank you very much for letting me borrow it. The language used in the book is actually very easy to understand!"

---

69. Kaplan, *The Gratitude Diaries*, 46.
70. Tracy, *No Excuses!*, Chapter 1.

"Yeah, that's what I think too. I was surprised when you said that the language seemed difficult," he said.

"I think the language in this book became easier as content became more meaningful and I became more familiar with the main concepts discussed in it," I explained.

Besides implementing the idea of making something meaningful in situations that were not very pleasant to me, such as my philosophy course, I also used that idea to motivate myself to do things when I was tempted to procrastinate or not prioritize them. Here are two examples of that.

Despite enjoying going to church on Sundays, there were times I was tempted to skip church so that I could get more work done. In other words, I wanted to prioritize my professional and academic lives over my spiritual life. However, the circle-of-life concept reminded me I should actually prioritize *all* areas of life. Therefore, to feel encouraged to attend church every Sunday (even if I had a great amount of work to do), I told myself that I couldn't miss it, because I needed to find out what meaningful message God had for me that day. As a result of seeing the act of going to church as a meaningful activity, I have left Mass with amazing messages, which only reinforce the ideas of this book—ideas that can lead us into the happiness pathway (regardless of whether we have a religion or not). Some of those messages are as follows:

- Take advantage of opportunities wisely; be grateful (Eph. 5:15–20).
- Get rid of negative feelings; be kind to others; forgive others (Eph. 4:31–32).
- Love with all your heart (1 Cor. 12:31–13:13).
- Take action to be a better person (Eph. 4:22–24).
- Be observant; make others feel special (Luke 10:38–42).

- If needed, ask for help and you will receive it; open your heart to happiness and forgiveness; be generous (Luke 11:1–13).
- Appreciate what is given to you; live peacefully (Luke 10:1–12).

The other example of making tasks more meaningful to encourage myself to accomplish them is creating a to-do list with names. As you already know, I love to check items off to-do lists. However, there are times that I need some extra encouragement to go through the whole list. Again, that's because sometimes I tend to prioritize other tasks. To motivate myself to accomplish all the little or not-so-little tasks on my to-do list, I started to write the name of the person related to each task. For instance, let's say I had to send the draft of a manuscript to my friend Wei and to invite Isabel to have lunch. Instead of writing the following on my to-do list:

- Send draft of the manuscript to Wei
- Invite Isabel for lunch

I would write the following:

- Wei—send draft of the manuscript
- Isabel—invite for lunch

This tiny change in how I wrote my to-do lists brought a whole different meaning to them. What once was considered mundane became meaningful because the items from the lists were related to other people (or myself). Having in mind that I care about others and should be kind and respectful to others' needs, I started finding my to-do lists very meaningful. In the end, I was motivated to accomplish all the items listed on them.

Making my actions meaningful encouraged me to accomplish them and boosted my motivation, creativity, energy, productivity, and, consequently, happiness.

Controlling Anxiety

Jeremy Bennett, the author of *The Power of the Mind*, argued that, contrary to what many people believe, situations don't cause anxiety. Instead, our *reactions* to situations cause anxiety.[71] That's why the presence of a certain person can make someone feel excited, whereas the same person can make someone else feel stressed. That's also why an action, such as flying on a plane, can make someone feel relaxed and make someone else feel nervous. Bennett's point was that we can therefore control our anxiety. Great news! But the question is: *How* can we control anxiety? Together with strategies to lower anxiety that I learned from other experts, I decided to test Bennett's argument. My statistics oral exams were the perfect opportunity for me to test all I had learned so far about controlling my anxiety.

As I stated in the beginning of this chapter, in the spring semester I took another statistics course with the same professor, Dr. James, a well-known, internationally distinguished professor. In that second statistics course, he assessed his students' learning through two oral exams. On the day of the statistics midterm oral exam, I decided to put into practice some techniques I had learned to control stress and feel confident during a challenging situation. Three of the techniques were *smile, do a high-power pose*, and *think about the challenges I have already successfully faced in life*. Before going into the details about how I applied those techniques, let me explain how they control anxiety.

Research shows that our bodies impact our thoughts and feelings. Therefore, we can take advantage of that and use our bodies to control

---

71. Bennett, "The Amazing Power of Your Mind."

our minds. For example, researchers such as Achor, Ben-Shahar, and Lyubomirsky encourage us to use the act of a smile as a technique to not only make us feel happier but also help us control anxiety.[72] As they explain, when we smile, our brains release dopamine and oxytocin, among other chemicals that help us perceive situations as positive, improve our mood, reduce negative feelings, and create happy moments. Moreover, smiles have the potential to increase our emotional and social intelligence.

Another evidence of how our bodies can impact our minds is through high-power poses. In her TED Talk, "Your Body Language May Shape Who You Are," social psychologist Amy Cuddy said that "our bodies can change our minds; our minds can change our behavior, and our behavior can change our outcomes." For example, her study findings indicated that people felt more powerful after doing a high-power pose (i.e., a pose that makes people bigger by spreading their arms or legs, such as raising their arms in a victory pose) for a couple of minutes. That is, people's levels of confidence, comfort, assertiveness, optimism, and risk taking increased, which resulted in good performance during a stressful situation.

As Cuddy explained, high-power poses lead to powerful feelings because they raise the level of testosterone, a dominance hormone, and decrease the level of cortisol, the stress hormone.[73] Therefore, she encouraged people to power pose in a private place (e.g., a bathroom) for two minutes to control their anxiety and be themselves, especially when they have to go through evaluative situations, such as speaking in public or having a job interview.[74] She also encouraged her viewers to "share the science" in order to help others. So following her suggestion, besides

---

72. Achor, *Before Happiness*; Ben-Shahar, *Choose the Life You Want*; Lyubomirsky, *The How of Happiness*.
73. Cuddy, "Your Body Language May Shape Who You Are."
74. Ibid.

applying her technique, I have shared it with others, including Vitor, my eleven-year-old nephew.

While visiting my family in Brazil, a few days after I explained the benefits of power posing to Vitor, he said, "Aunt Angelica, I raised my arms in a victory pose for two minutes yesterday before I took a test at school."

Surprised, I proudly asked, "Really?"

"Yeah!" he answered with a big smile while my parents and brothers looked puzzled and lost in the conversation.

After sharing the science with my family, I asked, "So, Vitor, did the high-power pose help you?"

"Yes! The test was so easy!" he said confidently.

Feeling very happy and proud of him for following my advice, I said, "Wow! That's awesome, Vitor! Now you know what to do anytime you want to increase your confidence to face something difficult. By the way, where did you power pose? Did you go to the bathroom?"

"No. I raised my arms for two minutes in the classroom," he replied.

"Didn't your teacher think you had a question to ask before the test?" I asked, thinking of when I was a teacher.

To my surprise, he said, "No, she didn't."

Knowing that our minds can change our behavior, in his book *Before Happiness*, Achor suggested that one way to face a challenging moment is to remind ourselves of other successes or, as he called them, "champion moments" we have accomplished in life.[75] Thinking about challenges we have already overcome makes us stronger and reminds us of our potential to face obstacles successfully. As a result, we feel more energetic, positive, confident, and motivated to go through the challenges.

Having those three techniques in mind (i.e., smile, do a high-power pose, and think about the challenges I have already successfully faced in

---

75. Achor, *Before Happiness*, Skill 3, Strategy 2.

life), let me go back to my statistics oral exam as an example of a stressful evaluative situation when I needed to control my anxiety.

Since the oral exam was going to be with that particular professor, Dr. James, I needed to apply all of those techniques and more. Here is a little background for you to better understand why I needed to arm myself with several antianxiety techniques.

I had already heard that several students felt intimidated by Dr. James's presence during the exam. The way they felt negatively impacted their performance during the exam; several students' grades ended up not reflecting their true learning. Many of his students also felt intimidated in his lectures, when they were not even taking exams. Maybe that was why students did not participate much in his classes. Besides, every time someone answered a question in class, he would informally assess the correctness of the answer and confidence of the student in giving the answer. So, many times, Dr. James said to different students, "A for correctness. D for confidence!" or "A for correctness. F for confidence!" Very few times, he said, "A for correctness. B for confidence!" I can't remember hearing any "A for correctness. A for confidence!" Maybe he applied that informal assessment as a joke. But if it was the case, Dr. James was very good at sarcasm.

In one of the assignments on regression, I tried to give him a hint on his tough teaching style. In the assignment, I had to come up with a dependent variable and three predictors. The goal was to identify if the three predictors correlated with the dependent variable, and if so, how much they uniquely and commonly (two or three predictors combined) correlated with the dependent variable. Well, since the assignment allowed me to be creative, I chose *happiness* as the dependent variable and the following three predictors: *social connections, acts of kindness*, and *kind professors*. Then, I randomly entered made-up data for each predictor. I ran the regression analysis, and although real research shows that *social connections* are the best predictor for happiness, my fake research showed that *kind professors* best predict happiness. My results, of course, were not valid, but they suggested the hint I wanted to give to Dr. James. Unfortunately, my hint didn't work. In the following class, after he had already checked my assignment (which had no remarks about my predictors), there he was, looking very serious and intimidating, as usual.

Going back to the midterm oral exam, I felt confident about the content but uneasy about the idea that during the test I would not be allowed to take notes, except in the air, as my classmate Vanessa reminded me.

"Since he might ask us to compute different correlations, beta weights, sum of squares, and structure coefficients, I'm going to ask him if I can take notes on a blank piece of paper. Do you think he will allow me to take notes?" I asked Vanessa in our study group the day before the exam.

"Yes…" she said, making me happy to get a positive answer from her. Then, she continued, "But in the air."

"In the air?" I asked, very confused about her answer.

"Yes, he'll definitely allow you to use your finger and write whatever you want in the air," she said, based on a conversation she had with some of his previous students.

Knowing that I would not even be able to write any numbers down just increased my anxiety about the exam. During the exam, I had to be able to keep anxiety low while showing my confidence in answering the questions. But what could I do about that? Not being able to take notes during the exam was out of my control. I had to focus on what was in my control. So a few minutes before walking into Dr. James's office to take the oral exam, I decided to put into practice those three antianxiety techniques. I smiled, raised my arms in a victory pose as if I had won a big prize (I went to the bathroom for that, of course), and thought of challenges that were successes, such as job interviews. All those techniques together, with one more technique that I added when I walked into his office, seemed to have helped reduce my anxiety and keep my confidence level high.

To my surprise, when I saw Dr. James sitting down at his desk waiting for the next student (me), a fourth technique came to me. Without hesitation, I said to him, "Before we begin, I want to thank you for making me to go through this *unpleasant* situation." (Yes, you read it right. I did say *un*pleasant.) "It is when I am out of my comfort zone that I grow. So *thank you* for putting me in this very uncomfortable situation." Later that semester, I realized that I had just practiced a concept Tracy discussed in his book *No Excuses!* He argued that situations of discomfort make us grow, so he encouraged people to face their fears and take actions toward their goals.

"OK," he said with a smile. I wasn't expecting him to smile, because his students rarely saw him smiling. Dr. James's unexpected smile and my unexpected sign of gratitude helped put my anxiety aside and focus on the exam content. I answered everything he asked me and tried my best to show confidence in my answers. Fifteen minutes later, he said, "Very good. That's an A." As I heard that, I jumped up and down with joy. Of course, my whole up-and-down jumping was just in my mind. My joy wasn't as much for my grade as it was for proving to myself I was capable of controlling my stress and anxiety during a challenging situation.

During the exam, I had controlled my anxiety so well that when he asked, "Do you have any questions for me?"

I said, "No, but I have a beach to recommend to you." He looked confused. I continued, "The other day in class, you described the beautiful beach in Rio de Janeiro. I am from Brazil, but not from Rio de Janeiro. I'm from Fortaleza, which is also a beach city."

"Is it near Rio de Janeiro?" he asked, seeming interested in my recommendation.

"No. It's about three hours by plane. But since you are going to retire at the end of the semester and it seems that you really liked the beaches in Rio de Janeiro, I think you would like to visit a beach called Jericoacoara, which is in Ceara, the state where I am from."

"OK," he said with another smile.

Wow, I got him to smile twice in a span of fifteen minutes, I thought.

"Can I have a piece of paper so I can write down the name of the beach?" I asked as I remembered Vanessa saying that he would only allow me to write in the air. I wrote down *Jericoacoara* and described the beach to him. I told him many tourists from all over the world go there, and some of them never go back home because they fall in love with the place. He looked intrigued at what I was saying.

When I went back to my office, I sent him an e-mail with a link showing pictures of Jericoacoara. Minutes later, he replied saying, "Thank you. It looks quite stunning!"

After reading that short e-mail, I caught myself feeling very happy. Not only did I do well on the exam, but, unlike many students, I controlled my anxiety and didn't feel intimidated during the test.

My performance in the first oral exam gave me confidence for the final oral exam. However, I was still nervous as I walked up the stairs to the seventh floor, where the exam was going to take place. So I thought, *I should do the same techniques that I did in the midterm oral exam* (i.e., smile, power pose, and think about the challenges I have already successfully faced in life). But then, I decided to try something new to help me go through that challenging moment.

I remembered Ben-Shahar's words saying that it was OK to *be human* and *accept our feelings*.[76] He also said that we should choose to *be benefit finders*, meaning that we should look for something positive when going through difficult situations.[77] So instead of repeating the

---

76. Ben-Shahar, *Choose the Life You Want*, Choice 55, Choice 97.
77. Ibid., Choice 19.

techniques I used in the midterm oral exam, I decided to apply those new techniques: *be human, accept my feelings,* and *be a benefit finder.* Despite feeling confident in the exam content, I chose to accept the fact that I was nervous and to find a benefit in being so. And I did. As I looked at my Fitbit display, it gave me an idea.

When I walked into Dr. James's office, I said, "Thank you for not only one but *two unpleasant* moments," referring to the two oral exams with him. He smiled. Then I went on to say, "Dr. James, I have an idea for a study for you. Too bad you are retiring soon. But here's what you could do for a study if you weren't retiring: have your students wear one of these things"—I pointed at my Fitbit—"to check their heartbeats in order to know how they feel when they come to take the oral exam with you. Look at this—my heartbeat is one hundred twelve now!" That was definitely far from my average heartbeat, which was around sixty-six.

Showing that I was nervous was nothing new to Dr. James. By his comments in class, most, if not all of his students felt nervous taking his oral exams. I think he even enjoyed seeing his students out of their comfort zone because it indicated that they took his exams seriously. My purpose for sharing that study idea with him (i.e., to investigate how his students felt entering his office on the exam day) was to break the ice so that I could feel less nervous. In doing that, I not only accepted my feelings and found the benefit in being nervous, but I also used that benefit successfully. I say this because Dr. James laughed (it must have been the first time I saw him actually laughing) at the idea I gave him for a research study. His reaction immediately made me feel less nervous and ready to answer the exam questions. About ten minutes later, "That's an A," he said. I left his office proud of allowing myself to be human, accept my feelings, and find a benefit in a challenging situation.

Bennett was right. Situations don't cause anxiety. Our reactions to situations cause anxiety.[78] We just need to remember that our minds and

---

78. Bennett, "The Amazing Power of Your Mind."

bodies are interconnected, so by making use of simple techniques, we are able to control our behavior and thoughts.

Spreading the Word

In an interview, Rubin said that sometimes she felt she had to control herself not to become a happiness bully.[79] For example, when she noticed someone who was stressed, she would have to bite her tongue not to give any tips on how to avoid stress. The more I learned about happiness within positive psychology, the more I felt like her; the difference was that I would not bite my tongue. Here is an example of that. Throughout the spring semester, I witnessed several undergraduate students struggling to cope with their busy academic lives. As a result, their stress affected their health, relationships, and academic performance.

One day, an undergraduate student of mine shared that she was so overwhelmed with her job and all her schoolwork that she was sleeping only about four hours a day. After following that pattern for a few weeks, she started missing early classes because her body was exhausted and she had no energy to make herself get up in the morning. Consequently, her academic performance dropped, and she even "felt dumb sometimes" because she "couldn't think right," as she described it. Her stress also led her to become anemic, have skin rashes, and end a long-term relationship.

Similar to that student, there are many other people who cannot control the stress of their everyday lives, which negatively impacts their happiness and well-being. As Achor said, "Stress is inevitable, but its effects are not," meaning that we can do something to avoid its bad effects, such as fatigue and headaches.[80] Two main things that we can do to better deal with stress are to take self-responsibility and take action.

---

79. Rubin, "Don't Worry, Be Happy Now."
80. Achor, *Before Happiness*, Skill 1, Strategy 1.

Feeling stressed can be a result of choices we have made in our lives; therefore, we should take self-responsibility for our stress because we are the ones who make the choices in life. Also, we should take action to make a change to avoid feeling stressed. In his book *The Six Pillars of Self-Esteem*, Branden reminded us that "Nobody is coming." If we do not like something about our lives or about ourselves, *we* have to do something about it.

With all that in mind, I listened to my student as I kept thinking of how I could help her. I couldn't release her from any course assignments or dismiss her from some classes. It wouldn't be fair to her classmates, who were also having a busy semester. Additionally, I didn't want to help her just temporarily, because she no doubt would encounter other stressful moments later in life. I wanted to help her successfully overcome that overwhelming semester but also other similar moments. That said, I shared with her some of what I had learned about happiness and how to deal with stress. For example, I told her about the five brain exercises for lasting positive change that I had learned from Achor: (1) write down three gratitudes, (2) journal a positive experience, (3) do physical exercise, (4) meditate, and (5) do a random act of kindness.[81] I also shared the positive impact those exercises had on my life and the importance of taking action to change the way we feel. Moreover, I encouraged her to listen to audiobooks and YouTube videos on happiness.

My student listened to me attentively, but I wondered if she was skeptical of what I said to her. I couldn't blame her if she felt that way. I assume many other undergraduate students would be skeptical. Imagine the scene: An undergraduate student goes into the instructor's office to explain why she has several unexcused absences and why the quality of her academic work has declined. She is probably hoping the instructor makes some type of arrangement or accommodation to help her out. Instead, the instructor says that if she trains her mind to be more

---

81. Achor, "The Happy Secret to Better Work."

positive and feels happy now, she will improve her academic performance and other areas of her life. The instructor explains that as a result of her positive mind-set, she will start focusing on positive things, which will help her find solutions to problems and better deal with stressful moments. And then, to wrap up the conversation, the instructor basically "prescribes medication for happiness" by encouraging her to do five brain exercises for lasting positive change. Thinking that is still not enough, the instructor also "prescribes" the student some YouTube videos and audiobooks on happiness.

It's important to mention that the instructor (me) is not from a positive-psychology department, but from an education department. Having said that, if my student was skeptical of everything I told her, I couldn't blame her or be surprised about it. I'm sure the conversation I had with that student was very different from what she expected. Unfortunately, a month later, she came back to my office to give me explanations for the same issues; nothing had changed.

I know that, unfortunately, not everybody wants to put in the effort to be happier or believes that happiness can positively impact work performance (which could have been the case for that particular student). That experience made me ask myself, "Should I bite my tongue to avoid giving tips to people on what they should do to improve something about their lives in order for them to feel happier?" After some consideration, I answered my own question: "No, I need to keep trying to help others feel happier, but I should make my suggestions indirectly (or at least less directly) so I don't become a happiness bully."

A few weeks later, another undergraduate student came into my office. She was also feeling overwhelmed with everything that was happening in her personal and academic lives, leading her to disappointment and unhappiness. Having my new approach in mind—be less direct—I asked her, "Have you ever heard of the book *My Happiness Project*, by Gretchen Rubin?"

"No, I haven't," she replied.

"It's a book about this woman, the author of the book, who spent one year trying out things to make her happier," I said.

"It sounds interesting," she commented.

"It definitely is. I think you would like it, and you may even find it useful. I've read it. Well, actually, I've listened to it. You know, our semester is so busy that it's hard to find time to do extra reading. But, anyway, that book has helped me be a much happier person. For example, I learned that we can create happiness by doing things we take for granted, like having a good night of sleep or a cup of coffee with a friend. Also, I learned our happy feelings contribute to how we deal with life issues."

She smiled, agreeing with what I was saying.

I don't know if that student bought *My Happiness Project* after our conversation, but a few days later, I received an e-mail from her saying:

Professor Ribeiro,

I appreciate you sharing your thoughts on happiness. Your kind words really helped me and continue to help me through this hard time.

Her words made me very happy because they showed I probably planted a seed in her mind about the importance of happiness.

Still trying to spread the word about happiness, toward the end of the semester, I started the class by asking my students to write down three things for which they were grateful. But to apply my less-direct approach on talking about happiness, I gave them the following warm-up question: *What are three good things that have happened to you this semester?* I was astonished to see that after writing two good things that happened to them, most students couldn't think of a third one! They were healthy, smart, and beautiful students who were attending a very good university; yet most of them couldn't think of three gratitudes to share. That made me decide to take a few minutes to open a discussion about that warm-up question. So I asked them, "Was it easy to think of three good things that happened to you this semester?"

One student said, "No! After writing two things, I couldn't think of anything else. But I could easily think of three bad things that happened to me."

After other students shared similar thoughts, I asked, "Why is it easier to think about the bad things as opposed to the good things that happen to us?"

One student said, "I think it's because we tend to forget the good things more easily than the bad ones."

Another student said, "I could actually think of three good things, but I hesitated to write them down because if I had to share them in class, other people could think I wanted to show off."

A different student added to that by saying, "Unfortunately, our society has taught us to focus on the negative, so if something very good happens to someone, we tend to think that person is trying to be better than others."

Then I asked, "How did you feel when you were thinking of the good things that happened to you this semester?" Without any hesitation, the students said they felt happy.

I went on to ask, "And how can happiness impact teaching and your future students' learning?"

A student said, "When students are happy, they tend to learn faster."

Another student added, "When students are happy, they are more open to learning."

"Happy students are more motivated to learn," a third student said.

After some other students shared more benefits of happiness in education, I added, "Happy students also tend to be more creative, take more risks, and, best of all, they spread their happiness to their peers. So the question is, what can you, as future teachers, do to make your students feel happier in the classroom?"

Among several answers my students gave to that question, one of them was, "We can do a warm-up like the one you did today—ask students to write down three good things that happened to them." I was happy to hear that particular answer because it showed that a simple classroom activity had brought happy feelings to many of my students, if not all of them. But, most importantly, by starting a class feeling good, my undergraduate students might pass on that experience to their future students.

I concluded that undergraduate course by showing Achor's TED Talk, "The Happy Secret to Better Work," in class to reinforce the idea that happiness can lead us to success. Inspired by psychologist Waldez Ludwig, who said that information doesn't have any value if it isn't spread, I keep sharing what I have learned about happiness whenever there is an opportunity; no wonder I decided to write this book.

Using Money for a Happy Purpose

Researchers such as Lyubomirsky argue that money makes us happy.[82] That *is* true, but the question is: Does money bring us short-term or long-term happiness? I had never given any thought to that question until I started my happiness journey. Although several happiness researchers and authors have an answer for that question, I wanted to find out for myself.

After reflecting on the connection between money and happiness throughout the spring semester, I concluded that the answer to that question—*Does money bring us short-term or long-term happiness?*—is: it depends. Based on my experience, money brings me short- or long-term

---

82. Lyubomirsky, *The How of Happiness.*

happiness depending on how I spend the money. I admit that, like many other women, I enjoy buying clothes, shoes, makeup, and purses, for example. However, I have noticed that those purchases only bring me short-term happiness. I get very excited when I buy them, but a few days later, they have little effect on my happiness; a few months later, many of them are even forgotten in the back of the closet. On the other hand, I have noticed that certain purchases contributed a lot to my long-term happiness because they helped me be healthier, more productive, more generous to others, more sociable, and more knowledgeable.

Here are a few examples of how money brought long-term happiness to me. One day, after feeling annoyed for being unable to concentrate on my studies because of all the noise around me when I was on campus, I decided to buy a Bose noise-cancelling headset. It wasn't cheap, but it was worth it! It has greatly contributed to my productivity, a main predictor for my happiness.

Other purchases that contributed to my lasting happiness were a portable DVD player and Tony Horton's *10 Minute Trainer*. In addition to being aware of the benefits of physical exercise, I really enjoy working out. Since I split my week between Houston and College Station, and I don't always have the time to go to the gym, I decided to exercise at home. So the purchase of a short and effective workout program, together with a portable DVD player, has allowed me to exercise every day, which makes me healthier and more energetic, improves my mood, and increases my productivity.

Spending money on others has also brought lasting happiness to my life. Since I started performing a daily act of kindness, I often catch myself thinking, *Who am I going to do something nice for today?* It is exciting to know that it is up to me to choose someone to make him or her feel happier (even if it is for a short period of time) through a simple act of kindness. Most of my acts of kindness don't involve money, but sometimes they do. For example, one day after surprising Vanessa, a friend who knew about my happiness journey, with a cake pop from Starbucks, she smiled and said, "Oh! Thank you! Am I your act of kindness victim of the day?"

"Yes, you are. So enjoy it!" I answered.

There were also times that my acts of kindness would make a much bigger impact on someone's life than I ever thought. For instance, one day I gave a small lunch bag to a colleague. She was very happy with the gift, but I think I was even happier, especially after seeing the impact that gift had on her. The lunch bag helped her change her diet for the better. She rarely took lunch to work because she only had a big lunch bag. In her mind, if she took the big lunch bag to work, her colleagues would assume that she had taken a lot of food to eat. So, very often, she ended up eating snacks from a vending machine. But after she got the small lunch bag, she started taking healthy lunches from home. By improving her diet, she improved her energy and mood, which led her to be more productive at work and to feel happier.

Spending money on social occasions has contributed to my long-term happiness as well. For example, every month, I have lunch with a couple of friends; every year, I make sure to visit my family in Brazil. I've realized the amount of money spent on social situations becomes irrelevant when compared to the joy I feel while interacting and sharing good moments with my friends and family.

Money spent on books and workshops has also contributed to my lasting happiness. For example, most of what I learned about happiness came from audiobooks. However, when I decided to write this book, I bought the same audiobooks again, but in book form so I could revisit their content more carefully. I also decided to be part of Vieira's workshop on emotional intelligence. That was the workshop I once told my friend Wladmir that I wouldn't attend because it was very expensive. About a year after I said that, I not only attended the workshop, but I also paid for a dear friend to attend it too. All the books and workshops were not cheap; however, they made me more knowledge-able about happiness and contributed to my well-being and personal growth. Moreover, I would probably not even be here writing this book on happiness or living a more mindful life if it weren't for what I learned from those resources.

In short, as many researchers argue, money does make us happy. However, it is up to us to spend money in a way that will bring us long-term happiness. To me, money brings long-term happiness when it contributes to others' well-being, as well as to my personal and profes-sional growth.

Saving Mental Energy

One good thing about my happiness journey was that it helped me real-ize what makes me happy. As a high achiever, I've learned productivity is definitely a source of happiness for me. It's easy to *define* the adjec-tive *productive*, but it's not that easy to *be* a productive person because it demands more than a great deal of discipline and determination. It requires good use of mental energy.

In his book *Before Happiness*, Achor pointed out that "the brain has a limited amount of resources"; therefore, we should use brain resources wisely.[83] Also, we should avoid wasting mental energy and make more brain resources available to us. After learning about the importance of brain resources and mental energy, the question became: What can I do to avoid wasting mental energy and make more brain resources available to me so that I can be more productive?

I learned that eating and sleeping regularly can help us free up brain resources and give us mental energy. That was good news because eat-ing healthily and sleeping were already part of my happiness journey. I made sure not to skip any meals and have snacks throughout the day so

---

83. Achor, *Before Happiness*, Skill 2, Strategy 3.

that I didn't feel hungry while studying, teaching, or attending classes and meetings. Avoiding feeling hungry not only helped me keep a good mood but also contributed to my thinking process, especially when I encountered situations in which I had to make important decisions or complete a challenging task, such as writing a research paper.

As for sleeping, I created the habit to, whenever possible, take a fifteen-minute nap (with no snooze) after lunch. It was amazing to see that only fifteen minutes made a big difference in my productivity. I'm sure it was because rest freed up some brain resources for me to reapply at work. According to Achor, eating and sleeping regularly help us have brain resources that call our attention to more valuable information, relevant details, and better solutions, thus making our realities more positive than if we didn't eat or sleep regularly.[84]

Another strategy I used to make more brain resources available was to take a short break during work. I learned about the importance of breaks from Goodson in her writing workshop and book *Becoming an Academic Writer*. She emphasized that we should take a fifteen-minute break after every forty-five minutes of writing. She added that we shouldn't feel we are wasting our time by doing that because our brains keep working for us when we take breaks. Goodson was right. After following her advice for about a year now, I have noticed that taking short mental breaks during work feels like hitting the reset button and making myself ready to continue working. That reset-button feeling indicated that more brain resources had become available to me through mental breaks. Not to mention that during my short breaks, my brain often lightened up with great ideas and clarity about my work.

Taking mental breaks also helps me avoid wasting mental energy. As Goodson explained, by working for many hours in a row, especially writing, we use up our brain resources, which leads us to experience fatigue, frustration, and lack of productivity. Furthermore, Achor pointed

---

84. Ibid., Skill 1.

out that small decisions, complaints, and worrying can make us waste mental energy.[85] He suggested creating habits so that we don't waste mental energy deciding if we should or shouldn't do something.

Only after learning about mental energy, I noticed that I wasted it on small decisions. For example, one morning I got up at five thirty, as usual. As I put on my gym clothes, I caught myself having this dilemma in my mind: *Even though it's time to get up (according to the schedule I created for me), should I go back to bed and sleep a little longer since I didn't sleep long enough, or should I exercise (which is how I start the day)?* Trying to find an answer based on what I had learned about the benefits of sleep and physical exercise, I thought, *What should I do? Sleep and exercise will both benefit me.* Then, the list of their benefits ran through my mind.

Researchers such as Achor, Lyubomirsky, and John Ratey report that physical exercise decreases anxiety and stress; increases optimism, confidence, quality of life, and happiness level; helps us control our weight and sleep better, build bones, joints, and muscles; and protects us from dementia, cognitive impairments, and several diseases, including cancer and diabetes.[86] On the other hand, sleep is very beneficial too. Research also indicates that seven to eight regular hours of sleep contribute to weight loss and happiness. However, lack of adequate sleep affects memory, learning, metabolism, and immune functions. As Lyubomirsky summarized, "If we don't obtain an adequate amount of sleep, we'll suffer in terms of our moods, energy, alertness, longevity, and health."[87]

What should I do, then? I really want to sleep more, but at the same time, I want to exercise, especially because I won't have time to do it later. Which would benefit me more: sleep or exercise? I wonder if there is a study out there based on that question, I thought. That was when I stopped and

---

85. Ibid.

86. Achor, *Before Happiness*; Lyubomirsky, *The How of Happiness*; Ratey, "Run, Jump, Learn!"

87. Lyubomirsky, *The How of Happiness*, Chapter 9, Happiness Activity No.12, Activity and Rest section.

said to myself, "Angelica, you're just wasting mental energy! Stick to your habits; get up at five thirty and exercise. Next time make sure to go to bed earlier so that you can have the benefits of both sleep *and* exercise." That day, I created the resolution *sleep for six and a half hours each night* (described in chapter 4). That experience made me realize the importance of habits as a way to avoid wasting mental energy. Therefore, besides the habits I have already created, I added a few more to keep my mental energy level high. For example, because the parking lot at Texas A&M University is very big and I would often forget where my car was parked, I started parking it at the same spot every time I went to the campus. I made sure to arrive there early in the morning before my chosen spot was taken. I also started planning my week on Sundays so that I didn't have to spend time or energy making decisions about what I had to do every day.

Complaints and worrying can also lower our brain resources and make us waste mental energy. Unfortunately, many times when we have to deal with unpleasant or challenging situations, we tend to spend a lot of brain resources on complaints and worrying as ways to try to get ourselves out of those situations. We tend to do that even before we try to turn those types of situations into successful accomplishments. However, complaints and worrying don't help us. On the contrary, they lower our mental energy, which we could be spending on actions and thoughts that move us toward achievements. Therefore, Achor suggested that we should focus our time and energy on brain resources that will help us reach success, and, consequently, be productive.[88]

I have witnessed several doctoral students, including myself, who complained about the amount of work that we were expected to do in a short period of time and without much support from professors. But I have learned that the time spent on complaining or even just thinking

---

88. Achor, *Before Happiness.*

about everything I had to get done filled me with anxiety and worry, and that wasted a lot of my mental energy. Therefore, since learning about the importance of mental energy, I have taken a different approach. Following Achor's advice, I avoid complaining and worrying; instead, I focus on what I can do to accomplish what needs to be accomplished.[89] Here is an example of a time I applied my new approach.

Remember Dr. James, my statistics professor? Well, it seemed that he was so aware of how challenging his courses were that he encouraged his students to study in small groups. Dr. James was also aware of his strict teaching style—lectures with limited visual aids and support from him. On the very first day of class in the fall semester (when I took the first statistics course with Dr. James), he said, "I've been teaching this course for over thirty years, so I know that when you meet with your study groups, you'll spend about two weeks just complaining about me. You'll say things like, 'How can he expect us to know how to do this assignment if he hasn't taught this content yet? He's such a bastard! He's this, he's that.' That's completely fine. But after two weeks, you'll realize that nothing will change, so you'll stop complaining and say, 'Let's suck it up and just learn this thing.'"

Dr. James was completely right. As he predicted, my study group, like many others, complained about him. But eventually we accepted his teaching style and focused on having productive study time. However, to my surprise, toward the end of the second statistics course taught by Dr. James in the spring semester, when several study groups met to review for the final oral exam, some students still complained about him! Not wanting to waste time or mental energy, especially because I really needed it, I said to those students, "You're still complaining about him? We stopped complaining last semester, after two weeks of classes. I think we should focus on what we can do, which is to get ready for the exam. Dr. James won't change, especially knowing that he's going

---

89. Ibid.

to retire at the end of this semester." Soon after I said that, the students stopped complaining, and we had a productive time reviewing for the test. I can't blame my colleagues for complaining, because that's what most people usually do when they face unpleasant or challenging situations. Unfortunately, many of them are unaware that they are simply misusing mental energy—energy they could be using for something that would actually bring them benefits.

In short, knowing that our brain resources are limited, I started using them the best way I could by applying habits and avoiding complaints, therefore saving mental energy and making more brain resources available to be used in what I wanted to accomplish. As a result, I was more productive, which translated into a higher happiness level.

Choosing Happiness Burgers

In his book *Happier*, Ben-Shahar described four types of burgers: Junk-Food Burger, Vegetarian Burger, Worst Burger, and Ideal Burger. The burgers represent our attitudes and behaviors in life that may or may not lead us to good feelings.[90]

The first burger type is called Junk-Food Burger. That's a tasty junk-food burger that we would enjoy eating but would regret it later. That is, the Junk-Food Burger represents our actions that bring present benefit but future detriment. To me, gossiping is an example of this type of burger. I have to admit that I enjoy gossiping, like many other people. Gossip brings me good feelings because I feel connected to the person I am talking to, but after leaving that situation, I feel awful and wish I could go back in time to choose not to gossip.

The second burger type is the Vegetarian Burger; a tasteless vegetarian burger that we wouldn't enjoy eating, but later we would feel happy for having eaten it. In other words, the Vegetarian Burger is actions we

90. Ben-Shahar, *Happier*, Chapter 2, The Hamburger Model section.

take that lead us to present detriment but future benefit. I experienced one particular example of a Vegetarian Burger throughout the spring semester. Every Tuesday and Thursday, I got up at 4:15 a.m. I decided to go to bed earlier in order to get up very early because I wanted to have time to fill out My Happiness Habit Journal, exercise, meditate, and write before the 8:00 a.m. class I had to teach. I know—4:15 a.m. is super early, and it didn't really bring happy feelings immediately, but it made me happy later in the day. So it was worth making that "sacrifice."

The Worst Burger is the third burger type. That's a tasteless and unhealthful burger that we wouldn't enjoy eating, and later we would regret having eaten it. The Worst Burger represents our behavior that brings present and future detriment. To me, an example of this type of burger is purposefully missing an opportunity to help someone. It makes me feel selfish and inconsiderate when I don't help others because I don't make the time or put in the effort to do so. Later, I feel even worse, wishing again that I could go back in time to make a better action choice.

Finally, the fourth type of burger is called the Ideal Burger, a tasty and healthy burger. We would enjoy eating it, and later we would feel good for having eaten it. Therefore, that burger or behavior gives us present and future benefit. In other words, the Ideal Burger represents happiness because, in Ben-Shahar's own words, "Happy people live secure in the knowledge that the activities that bring them enjoyment in the present will also lead to a fulfilling future."[91] Spending time with Kent and my family and friends definitely illustrates my Ideal Burger. The time I spend with them brings me happiness immediately and later.

The analogy of the four types of burgers has contributed a lot to my decision-making process. Whenever I am considering choices in any area of my life, I ask myself, "What type of burger represents this first choice? What about this second choice?" And so on. My goal, of course,

91. Ibid.

is always to decide on attitudes and actions that reflect the Ideal Burger or at least the Vegetarian Burger.

Choosing Positive Thoughts and Words

In his YouTube video ("The Amazing Power of Your Mind—A MUST SEE!"), author Bennett called our attention to how powerful our minds are and advised us to choose our thoughts wisely. According to him, our subconscious minds can't distinguish between reality and thoughts, which explains the placebo effect (i.e., the simple belief that an intervention will be successful). For example, research has shown that people were cured after taking sugar pills when they thought they were actually real pills. Contrary to the placebo effect, the nocebo effect shows that the mind actually contributes to sickness. In other words, because people believe they will get sick, they develop a disease in reality. Bennett then concluded, "Whatever belief you hold in your subconscious mind will become your reality."[92] It means that we are attracted to what we keep in our subconscious minds.

In the spring semester, I experienced an example of this notion that our thoughts can become our reality. For you to understand my experience, you should know that I am afraid of big dogs. I'm not sure why. It's probably because I didn't grow up around them. I feel so scared and uncomfortable around big dogs that I cannot even think right or carry out a decent conversation. As you can imagine, despite Kent's love for pets, we don't have dogs. For some reason, several times when I went to our backyard, I thought to myself, *Imagine if I ever saw a big dog in our backyard without Kent near me.* Well, I don't have to imagine it anymore. It really happened.

It was a Saturday morning; Kent was out playing soccer with his league team, and I was cleaning the house. When I opened the back

---

92. Bennett, "The Amazing Power of Your Mind."

door to take the trash out, I saw a big dog right behind the screen door. I had never been so grateful for screen doors! I could *not* believe what I was seeing. It actually took me a few seconds to realize that this was a real situation, not my imagination. Of course, I immediately closed the door as I tried to find out how that dog ended up in our backyard. The outside gate was closed and, as far as I could see, all the sides of the fence were up. Could the dog have jumped over the gate? I had no idea how it got there. And I had no idea what to do. I watched the dog from the window, and apparently it was having a blast. The dog ran and played in our backyard as if it was the best park ever. All of a sudden, I heard it crying. I assumed the dog wanted to either go back to where it belonged or play with me (because the dog kept looking at me through the window). I chose to believe it was the first option. Since Kent wasn't answering his phone, I called my friend Ivelina to help me. She came. But when we went outside to find the dog, it was gone.

"But the dog was right here!" I said, again questioning myself about whether it was a real or imagined situation. "Ivelina, I remember you telling me your dog jumped over your backyard gate one day. Do you think this dog could have done the same?"

"I don't know. Let's check the fence to see if there is something wrong with it," she replied.

Sure enough, we found a board in the fence that was rotted at the bottom, allowing the dog to push its way through. Needless to say, Kent and I fixed the fence right away. What was a scary situation to me was entertainment to Kent; he couldn't stop laughing at what had happened. Could the belief I held in my subconscious mind (the possibility that one day I could find a big dog in our backyard) have triggered that situation to become reality?

Tracy also discussed the power of our minds in his work on self-development. One of the examples he gave was about finding a parking spot in a very busy area. Based on the idea that our thoughts become reality, he said that if we truly believe we are going to find a parking spot, we do find it. I confess that at first I was skeptical of the idea that thoughts become our reality, but I was willing to give it a try, especially after the dog episode. One day, I went to a doctor's appointment and was surprised to see how packed the parking lot was. I looked at the clock in the car, and it showed that I had less than five minutes to park. Then, I thought, *Great! This is going to be a perfect opportunity for me to apply the power of my mind. I just have to believe that I will find a parking spot.* Since thoughts and language are connected, I kept thinking and saying out loud, "I will find a parking spot. I will find a parking spot. I have no doubt I will find a parking spot." Guess what? I could even choose where to park because I soon found three parking spots. It just happened that three people from three different cars were leaving at the same time. Amazing! I parked and still got to my appointment on time.

When I arrived home that day, I shared my mind-power experience with Kent. I had already told him about the idea that our thoughts become reality, but he didn't believe it, so I wanted to see if my story would change his beliefs.

"Honey, remember you said you didn't believe that thoughts become reality?" I asked.

"Yeah. What about it?" he said.

"Well, I wasn't sure if that was true either, but I'm starting to believe it," I said. Then, I excitedly told him about my parking-lot experience. As he listened to me, he smiled and nodded at what I said, but he wasn't convinced in the end. He still didn't believe that thoughts could become reality.

Then, he said, "Oh, I talked to someone from AAA today."

Since I frequently drive to College Station, knowing that we have the AAA services gives me peace of mind. So I had been bugging Kent to call AAA for weeks to provide them with some information they needed from him. "Really? Finally!" I gladly said. "Thank you! Did you call them?"

"No, they called me," he replied.

"They called you? See, that's the power of mind I've been telling you about! For weeks, you've been thinking about AAA, especially because I kept bugging you about it, and then you tell me that they called you. You just used your mind power! Now start thinking about Terminix," I said, referring to the pest-control company that Kent also had to call to provide them with some required information.

He laughed.

A few days later, I tried to convince Kent—and myself, I guess—about the power of mind again when he said, "It would be nice to get together with Ivelina's family this Saturday."

"Yes, it would," I agreed. Although we could have called Ivelina to make plans for the weekend, I chose to try our power of mind. So I suggested, "We should then start thinking that she will call to invite us over."

To my surprise, Kent accepted my suggestion. For the whole week, in our minds, we were certain that Ivelina was going to call us. We had even decided on the dessert to take to her house and crossed out any other possible plans for Saturday night because we were going to have dinner at her house.

Saturday morning came. Kent said, "She hasn't called."

"Maybe it's because *you* haven't been thinking hard enough. You've gotta believe it, honey! Think as if you *mean* it," I said in a joking tone.

When I looked at my phone a few minutes later, there was a missed call and voice message from Ivelina. She did invite us over, but for the following Saturday. When I told Kent about the call, he said, "What happened to this power of mind you talk about?"

"Don't you see that it happened? She did call! She did invite us to have dinner with them on Saturday. Maybe we just didn't emphasize enough in our thoughts that we wanted to see her family *this* Saturday," I said.

Could my thoughts have led me to find a parking spot and receive Ivelina's call? I'm still not 100 percent sure. But I do agree with the idea that when we think positively, positive things happen to us. Besides, negative thoughts just harm us. Negative thoughts, in Bennett's own words, "release cortisol (the stress hormone) into your blood, which then weakens your immune system, inhibits the actions of your white blood cells, increases the chances of infection and even promotes weight gain."[93] Therefore, we have to be careful with what we feed our minds so that we don't negatively impact our thoughts. With that said, I have chosen to think and speak positively. I even placed a little sticky-note reminder on my computer and phone that reads, "Think and speak positive things for only twenty-four hours."

Achor also supports the importance of using positive language because our words and actions impact how we feel.[94] My happiness-journey experience provided me with many examples illustrating that positive language does impact my feelings. For example, after I incorporated the tiny habit *After I touch my face, I will say, "I am assertive and confident,"* I did feel assertive and confident by repeating that affirmation every time I touched my face. As Branden explained, affirmations not only change how we feel, but by repeating them, we imprint the belief expressed through the affirmation in our minds.[95] The result of using positive language through affirmations was that now I have no doubt that I am assertive and confident; I don't have to repeat that affirmation anymore, because those qualities are already ingrained in my mind and how I feel about myself.

---

93. Ibid.
94. Achor, *The Happiness Advantage*, Principle #2, More Than 24 Hours in a Day? section.
95. Branden, *The Six Pillars of Self-Esteem*.

Another example of positive language came from my dissertation work. As I wrote the first draft of this chapter, I was working on another systematic literature review, one that would be part of my dissertation. After following a standardized search and procedures required by that type of review, I ended up with ninety-seven articles to read, code, summarize, and synthesize for my preliminary exam (the first phase of the dissertation process). Instead of thinking, *Wow, ninety-seven articles are a lot! They're going to require a lot of work and time!* I chose to think what I later told Kent: *You know what? I'm actually glad that I found ninety-seven articles, because after reading and coding all of them, they will make me confident to write and present my preliminary exam paper. Those articles will also help me with future research projects.*

So I downloaded all ninety-seven articles and saved them in a folder that I named "Hang in there. That is it!" to remind me to have patience and that those articles were the remainder of what I had to read to complete my dissertation (at least its literature-review section). I started reading them, and every time I finished an article, I moved it to a folder called "Woo-hoo!" to represent a little celebration in getting one more article done and motivate me to keep working hard on that review. Moreover, when Kent asked me, "How many more articles do you have to read?" I replied, "Only ninety-five more." Days later, I said, "Only eighty-nine articles left to read." As I wrote the first draft of this chapter, I only had twenty-five articles left. I realized that the simple fact that I chose to say the word *only* and the belief that the knowledge I gained from all those articles would increase my confidence in my field of study made me see this situation as a challenge. Seeing this situation as a challenge as opposed to a threat would benefit me in the near future and help me reduce my anxiety and my feelings of being overwhelmed.

In summary, I've been applying the idea "Think positively and positive things will happen to you" and following Bennett's advice to

"Choose your thoughts wisely."[96] As either a direct result of my thoughts and words or not, good things have happened to me. For example, in the spring semester, I was one of the few doctoral students invited to be part of a hiring committee and to participate in a root-cause analysis project. Also, I was offered a teaching position in higher education, and I doubled the number of Japanese students for me to tutor. Moreover, my graduate assistantship was renewed, which I didn't expect, since assistantships at the department where I study usually last only three years (as I wrote this chapter, I was about to start my fourth year in the program). I didn't expect any of those good things to happen. They simply happened! To me, that's an indication that we should not underestimate how much positive thoughts, words, and attitudes matter.

Accepting Ourselves

I have never given much attention to when people said to me, "You should just accept who you are and be yourself." However, my happiness journey made me reflect on the idea of accepting who we are. After giving a lot of thought to it, I have come to the following conclusion: yes, we should accept ourselves, but with some considerations. Keeping in mind that growth can lead us to happiness, we should not accept personality traits that do not contribute to our growth. In my case, my personality traits that were holding me back from growing as a person and professional were my lack of self-esteem, confidence, and assertiveness. As Branden said in his book *The Six Pillars of Self-Esteem*, high self-esteem, which is associated with confidence and assertiveness, is essential because it makes us more persistent in difficult times, gives us courage to take risks, helps us face obstacles, makes us feel more comfortable around people, improves the way we express ourselves, picks us up when we fall, and fills us with a desire to learn more and more.

96. Bennett, "The Amazing Power of Your Mind."

Therefore, I couldn't accept the lack of those traits in myself. That's why I took action to replace them.

On the other hand, we should accept our personality traits that can contribute to our growth. Therefore, we sometimes have to take action to stop resisting some of our own traits; instead, we should accept them by seeing the benefits they bring into our lives. In other words, if we change our perspective on those traits, we change the reality we see in them. Here's an example to better explain that we should accept positive characteristics that are already within us, but we may resist them or may not be aware of them.

Do you remember that I couldn't fully accept the fact that Rubin's Four Tendencies quiz revealed that I am an Obliger when I really wanted to be an Upholder? (If you recall, an Obliger is someone who meets outer expectations but resists inner expectations, while an Upholder is someone who meets outer and inner expectations.) Because I didn't want to accept my tendency (or the fact that I resist inner expectations), I did my very best to become an Upholder. After a few months putting into practice several new habits as an effort to be an Upholder, I said to myself, "Why has it been so hard for me to become someone who attends to outer and inner expectations? Why don't I want to be an Obliger, anyway? Is it bad to be an Obliger? I know that I wanted to be an Upholder, but I've never stopped to consider the benefits of being an Obliger." Using the questioning strategy, the more I reflected on the qualities of an Obliger (compared to an Upholder), the more I realized the benefits I would actually gain from being an Obliger. First, like an Upholder, being an Obliger helps me grow personally and professionally—one of my sources of happiness. Second, since Obligers like to please others, it allows me to perform acts of kindness—another source of happiness. Third, because Obligers have a hard time saying no to others, it provides me with more opportunities to practice my new assertive skills—skills that contributed to my growth and, consequently, my happiness level. Finally, some Obligers' characteristics overlap with Upholders' ones because both tendencies meet outer expectations. That means that my primary tendency may not be an Upholder, but I still have some Upholder qualities, such as my discipline, hard work, and determination.

In the end, by changing my perspective on what it meant to be an Obliger, it became clear to me that it was OK to be an Obliger and I should accept it because it brings me benefits, including sources of happiness. So now I fully accept the fact that I am an Obliger. Later in the spring semester, I listened to Rubin's interview on *The One Thing Webinar*, in which she said she believed it was very difficult, if at all possible, for people to change their given tendency. No wonder I couldn't change my Obliger tendency to the Upholder tendency. I'm glad I didn't listen to that particular interview earlier, because it was my desire to become an Upholder that drove me to new habits and more knowledge about happiness.

Another example of accepting something about me after changing my perspective on it was my role as a tutor. One day during the fall semester, my mother-in-law introduced me and Kent to some of her friends.

"This is my son, Kent. He's a professor at the University of Houston–Clear Lake, and this is Angelica, his wife. She's a tutor," she said.

Tutor? I thought. I couldn't even remember her friends' names because all my brain resources got stuck on the word *tutor* while they introduced themselves. Thinking of the hard work I was putting into the doctoral program, which also included teaching undergraduate courses, I couldn't believe all that was replaced by a temporary job I did one day a week. I was so blind to the benefits of my role as an English-as-a-second-language tutor that as soon as my mother-in-law's friends left, I used my brand-new assertive skills and said to her, "I do a lot more than just tutoring, which is a side job at the moment. My main job is being a doctoral student; the university even pays me to teach and assist other professors. So next time you mention what I do, could you please also say I am a doctoral student and instructor?"

"Sure! I'm sorry about that," she replied with a genuine smile, showing she had no intention to hurt me.

It was only a few months later that it dawned on me how much I should appreciate my role as a tutor. Before telling you more about this, I should mention that I strongly believe we should speak the official language of the country where we live, whether it's our home country or not. One day, I made that clear to a cousin of mine who had lived in New York for about ten years and still didn't speak much English. I said to him, "I know you live in a neighborhood where there are a lot of Brazilian people around, but still, you should learn English. What if someday you get in a car accident? How are you going to argue, negotiate, and come to an agreement?"

"You know, the other day, I did have a car accident," he said.

"Oh my! What happened? How did you communicate with the person who was driving the other car?" I asked.

"The guy from the other car was from Portugal. So we spoke in Portuguese, of course," he answered with a big smile on his face.

"What? From Portugal? How lucky! But anyway, I still think you should learn English," I insisted.

Having said that, I apply those same beliefs to my tutoring students—children and adults. I want them to be proficient in English so they will be able to express themselves and not depend on translators or limit their abilities due to language issues.

The realization of the importance of being a tutor happened at the end of a tutoring session when my student, whom I will call Fumiko, said, "Angelica, thank you for your lesson. I feel more confident now." The ironic thing was that I made her feel more confident when I myself was still going through the process of building my own confidence. *It's not easy to teach confidence, so I must have been doing something right,* I thought. That was when I stopped to reflect on my role as a tutor. I then realized I wasn't just teaching my students the English language; embedded in my teaching (based on conversations), I also was empowering them while encouraging them to be risk takers and live happier lives.

For example, I empowered Fumiko when I told her that she should speak up or question when she didn't understand something. At the time, she volunteered as a biologist at a national park, where she had to follow her supervisor's orders. Although Fumiko was able to express herself in English, she didn't feel it was appropriate to question or ask her supervisor for clarifications. As a result, her supervisor wasn't confident in Fumiko's work, because Fumiko was not completely following her instructions as expected. Of course, Fumiko wasn't doing what was expected of her! She didn't fully understand the instructions she received. I'm sure Fumiko's behavior can be explained by her Japanese culture, where most people don't question others who are in a higher position than theirs. So I said to her, "Fumiko, we should definitely keep and nurture our culture because it's part of our identity. But when necessary, we have to step out of our culture; otherwise, we may be misjudged. In your case, if you don't say something to your supervisor to make sure you understand her instructions, she will think (or maybe she already thinks) that you are not capable of doing or don't have the required knowledge to do what you are supposed to. I know you are more than capable of doing whatever she asks of you. You have a doctoral degree in biology! You may not think your English skills are good, but they are. You just have to speak up."

Fumiko didn't say much about what I told her, but she did start asking questions and speaking up at her volunteer job. Nowadays, she even gives lectures to schoolchildren who visit the park.

The following example shows how I encouraged another Japanese student, Makiko, to be a risk taker. In one of our tutoring sessions (which were in English), Makiko, who was a beginning English speaker, told me that she felt uncomfortable when her husband went on business trips.

"Why do you feel uncomfortable when he leaves?" I asked.

"Because I am afraid…if my son needs a doctor, I can't make an appointment," she answered.

"Why can't you make an appointment?" I asked.

"Because I don't know English. So people won't understand me," she replied.

"Makiko, you *do* know English. You may not know how to say in English everything you want, but you know enough English to talk to people and be able to make a doctor's appointment," I said.

"No, I don't," she said.

"Yes, you do. But since you don't believe me, let's practice. Let's pretend I am a doctor's office receptionist. Now, call me to make an appointment. Don't be afraid to make mistakes. Focus on communicating what you want to say," I told her.

So we role-played that situation several times. A few weeks later, when I walked into Makiko's house, she excitedly said, "I made a doctor's appointment by myself this week."

"You did? See, I knew you could do it! Now you don't have to depend on your husband to make appointments," I said. I felt very proud of her!

Here's one more example of how I positively impacted my tutoring students. One day, my student Akemi said, "Now that I am getting older, I accept everything, even if it's something I don't like or it's not going to make me happy."

I asked, "Why do you do that? And by the way, you're still very young. You're in your early forties!"

"Because I don't want to argue. It's easier just to say yes to people, especially to my husband and kids."

"Akemi, I understand that you don't want to spend your energy arguing with others, but you shouldn't do things that you don't like or accept everything people say to you; otherwise, you won't be fully happy."

In a not-very-convincing tone, she said, "I know."

On my last tutoring session with Akemi before she moved back to Japan, I gave her the book *The Happiness Project* and said, "I am giving you this book because I want you to be as happy as you can be. Live a happy life!"

With an emotional look and tone of voice, she said, "You just gave me a gift that I will treasure."

Although I still hope my mother-in-law remembers to give me credit for my hard work as a doctoral student, now I see the value of being a tutor. I couldn't have been able to identify those examples as evidence of how I positively impacted my Japanese students if I hadn't allowed myself to change my perspective on my role as a tutor. As Achor said, when we change our perspective, we change our reality, which can make a huge positive impact on our happiness.[97]

Forgiving Others

Last but not least, I would like to share one more lesson I learned throughout my happiness journey: to forgive others, that is, to let go and forget resentment against others—something I had struggled with. Forgiveness is a choice. As Ben-Shahar mentioned in his book *Choose the Life You Want*, we can either "hold a grudge or forgive."[98] When we choose to hold a grudge, we prevent our emotions from flowing. On the other hand, when we choose to forgive, we decide to unclog our

---

97. Achor, *Before Happiness*.

98. Ben-Shahar, *Choose the Life You Want*, Choice 8.

emotions and let our feelings flow. As a result, we open ourselves for, in Ben-Shahar's words, a "lighter, calmer, and happier" life.[99]

I know that to forgive is one of those things that is easier said than done, but the benefits we gain make it worthwhile to try to forgive, especially when it involves someone we care about and want to be part of our lives. We don't necessarily need to explicitly express our forgiveness out loud to benefit from it. I realized the benefits of forgiveness one day in the spring semester after bumping into someone I was still upset with for something that had happened months before. Driven by my commandment that says *let it go*, I simply chose to greet and chat with her for a little bit. After we said good-bye, I was amazed to notice how light and glad I felt. I never said anything to her about forgiveness; however, my decision to put my negative feelings toward her aside as a sign of forgiveness made me feel good because I replaced them with harmony.

The act of forgiveness supports the idea that our thoughts matter. For instance, Achor suggested we journal one positive experience we had in the last twenty-four hours, as an exercise for us to achieve a lasting positive change.[100] He explained that by writing down about a pleasant experience, we relive that moment, because our thoughts take us back to what happened. Consequently, it brings back the same good feelings we had while it happened. The same logic applies to anger or a grudge we may hold within us. Those negative feelings make us think and subsequently relive the situation that caused them. In other words, by holding grudges, we not only ruin relationships, but we can also harm ourselves due to the stress hormone that negative thoughts release into our bodies. Additionally, choosing not to forgive holds us back, as our thoughts keep taking us to the past. Instead, we should move forward in life by letting go of resentments we may have. Such attitude will open our hearts and minds to positive emotions and thoughts.

---

99. Ibid.
100. Achor, "The Happy Secret to Better Work."

It was after I learned how important forgiveness is for lasting happiness that I realized that only then I had fully *run into happiness* and therefore could finish writing this book.

Final Thoughts

My happiness journey was enhanced with the implementation of the ideas I shared in this chapter—*finding sources of happiness, making something meaningful, controlling anxiety, spreading the word, using money for a happy purpose, saving mental energy, choosing happiness burgers, choosing positive thoughts and words, accepting ourselves,* and *forgiving others.* Together with what I had already learned the semester before (e.g., strategies for an extraordinary life, brain exercises, tiny habits, resolutions, and my commandments), putting into practice what I learned in the spring semester taught my neurons to follow the positive pathway in my brain. As a result, I changed my mind about the world as I learned to see and experience it through a different perspective—a perspective based on optimistic beliefs and positive views of different life situations. My neurons were certainly keeping me on the right path—the path for happiness.

I chose *Running into Happiness* as the title of this book because I wanted to share with you how I "accidentally" learned how to create happiness in my life. Running into happiness doesn't mean I will be forever happy. However, my journey taught me what pathway I have to take for lasting happiness. Now it's up to me to choose thoughts, words, and actions that will keep me on the right path for happiness. Having said that, I have created My Happiness Habit Journal to help me stay on the lasting-happiness path and help you do the same.

WHAT ABOUT YOU?

- *Knowing that happiness can come from something meaningful, pleasurable, unpleasurable, and challenging, what are your sources of happiness? More specifically, what is something (a) meaningful, (b) pleasurable, (c) unpleasurable, and (d) challenging that can make you happy?*
- *How can you make one of your duties or activities meaningful to you?*
- *In which situations can you apply the following techniques to control your anxiety: smile, do a high-power pose, and think about the challenges that you have already successfully overcome in life?*
- *Which kind of messages do you usually spread to others: positive or negative messages? How do you feel after spreading those messages?*
- *Does money bring you happiness? If so, how? Does it bring you short- or long-term happiness?*
- *How do you use your mental energy? What would you do to save some mental energy and free up more brain resources?*
- *Which type of happiness burgers have you been choosing in your life: (a) Junk-Food Burger (actions that bring you present benefit but future detriment), (b) Vegetarian Burger (actions that bring you present detriment but future benefit), (c) Worst Burger (actions that bring you present and future detriment), or (d) Ideal Burger (actions that bring you both present and future benefit)?*
- *Which type of happiness burgers would you like to keep choosing in your life?*
- *Which type of thoughts and words do you usually choose to have: positive or negative? What have they attracted into your life?*
- *Do you have any personality traits that do not contribute to your growth? If so, what personality traits can you replace them with to help you grow as a person and a professional?*

- *What are two of your personality traits that already contribute to your growth? How do they contribute?*
- *How can you apply the act of forgiveness in your life?*

Seven

INTRODUCING MY HAPPINESS HABIT JOURNAL

My biggest lesson from my happiness journey was that we don't have to wait for happiness to come. I learned that we shouldn't think that we can be happy only if something special happens or that we can't be happy if we are faced with an unpleasant or challenging situation. I learned that we can create our own happiness through meaningful choices. My happiness journey helped me become aware that it is up to me to make choices of behavior, thoughts, words, and attitudes to boost my happiness. Such realization came not only from the books I read and videos I watched, but also mainly from putting into practice what I learned from them. As Achor said, "Information alone doesn't cause transformation."[101] I definitely agree with his statement, because before this journey, I had already read some self-help books, and none of them helped me. However, the lack of changes in my life wasn't because of those particular books. I didn't experience any change by reading self-help books in the past because I didn't put into practice the knowledge I gained from them. In contrast, my new-me journey or my happiness journey focused on actually implementing what I learned

---

101. Achor, *The Happiness Advantage*, Principle #6, Sleep in Your Gym Clothes section.

from researchers and experts on happiness and related topics. The fact that I turned new knowledge into new habits led me to be able to create long-term happiness in my life.

During the process of creating new habits that led me to a happier life, I created My Happiness Habit Journal. That journal not only helps me keep my habits alive, but more importantly, it also reminds me that I can create my own happiness through actions, thoughts, and words that I choose in my everyday life. As my mother says, "Our lives are a result of our decisions"; therefore, it is up to us to make choices in life that will lead us to feeling happy.

One day, while talking with one of my aunts on FaceTime, I noticed that she was being very negative. Her negative attitude was surprising, because she is often very positive. So after listening to one more negative comment, I asked her, "Aunty, can I ask you some questions?"

"Sure," she answered.

Based on the components of My Happiness Habit Journal, I asked her questions about gratitude, happy moments, kindness, and sources of happiness. "What's something meaningful that brings you happiness?" I asked her.

"Being close to my husband is something meaningful that brings me happiness," she answered.

"What about challenging? What's something challenging that makes you happy after you do it?"

"Cleaning the house and trying to get rid of some things I have," she said.

"What's a happy moment you experienced today?" I asked.

"A happy moment I had today was being at the carnival party," she replied.

"What is something you are grateful for?"

"I'm grateful for a tuna pie I had today. It was delicious!"

After answering several questions from My Happiness Habit Journal, my aunt said she felt 50 percent happier than before I asked her the questions. It was amazing to see how much happier she looked and sounded as a result of spending a few minutes reporting positive actions and feelings. That experience indicated that words and thoughts *can* change how we feel and that it doesn't take much time for that to happen. It is just a matter of focusing on words and thoughts related to how we want to feel. In this case, I wanted my aunt to focus on positive actions and feelings she experienced that day to encourage her to reduce her negativity and to create a positive mind-set—and she did.

I also used My Happiness Habit Journal with a cousin of mine. After personalizing the journal with her own commandments, resolutions, tiny habits, and goals for each component of the circle of life, I asked her to fill it out for three weeks. When I talked to her four days after she started using the journal, I asked her, "Bel, are you feeling happier as a result of filling out the journal?" I didn't really expect her to say *yes* because she had not even applied all the journal components for a full week yet.

"Happier? No, I don't think *happier* is the right word to describe how I feel. I am feeling…" She paused as she searched for the right word to express her feelings. "Happier," she said with a smile. "Yes, I *am* feeling *happier*. I think it's because I started doing habits that I've always wanted to do but never pushed myself to do them. So now that I know that at the end of the day I will fill out the journal and check the habits I did, it encourages me to follow through the new habits I set for myself. Then, seeing my habits and goals checked off makes me feel I have accomplished something. For example, making my bed gives me that accomplished feeling."

After using My Happiness Habit Journal for a little over three weeks, I approached Bel again and asked her if the journal had impacted her life at all.

"Yes, I developed habits I didn't have before, like making the bed. Also, the journal helped me notice small good things and attitudes I didn't notice before. For example, my brother and I share a car. One day this week, I couldn't use the car because he had to use it. But then, for some reason, he didn't have to leave the house anymore that day, so the car was available to me. Before using the journal, I wouldn't have noticed that situation made me happy. But after I started filling out the journal, I realized that being able to use the car was one of my happy moments that day."

"Bel, would you recommend the happiness journal to other people?" I asked her.

"Yes, I would. But they should be determined people who can create the habit of using the journal daily," she said. Then she added, "That journal is a good determination and commitment exercise," implying that even if the people who choose to use the happiness journal are not determined or committed, the journal can help them develop those character traits.

An undergraduate student of mine used My Happiness Habit Journal as well. After agreeing to use it for at least three weeks, she personalized it with her own commandments, resolutions, tiny habits, and goals for each component of the circle of life. At the end of the semester, she e-mailed me the following.

Good Afternoon Ms. Ribeiro,

I know I didn't get the chance to set a date and time to meet with you but I wanted to give you a quick run through of my journey with the happiness journal.

I was able to complete a month and my happiness went through the roof. I was calm and able to change any poor situation into a lesson learned or a happy moment. It really changed my perspective.

With life getting a little busy, I wasn't able to keep up with the practices the next month. My happiness didn't change as quickly as a flip of switch, but gradually changed. The past month, my anxiety has crept up with a vengeance. In the past month, I have experienced five anxiety attacks that have left my family concerned for my mental health.

What I've learned is that if I don't take the time to take care of myself and my happiness, my anxiety peaks. During the last attack, I learned how to get it under control. Out loud I had to repeat my commandments. It distracted me from my panic of the way I feel and redirected my focus to the good things I know are true.

I truly have to say thank you for opening the door for me. I will definitely be spreading your ideas of kindness and happiness. Please let me know when you release your book, I will definitely be purchasing it.

Eternally grateful,
Sharitza

My student's e-mail was one of my happy moments that day. I had no words to describe how rewarding it was to know that My Happiness Habit Journal helped her realize how to control anxiety and create more happiness in life. Her e-mail reinforced the idea that I had to go on with this book—publish it as a way to touch other people's lives.

I have incorporated some components of My Happiness Habit Journal in my undergraduate classes. The students seemed to enjoy addressing the happiness-related components in class. One particular student, who was a restaurant manager at the time, started doing the same thing with his employees. At every work meeting, he took some time to implement a few of the components of My Happiness Habit Journal with the employees. He told me he was amazed to see how much such practice improved the employees' happiness levels, and, consequently, their work performance and customer satisfaction.

Why You Should Use My Happiness Habit Journal

As Lyubomirsky alerted us in her book *The How of Happiness*, the difference among people's happiness can be explained by their genetic makeup (50 percent), life circumstances (10 percent), and behavior (40 percent).[102] It indicates that we may not be 100 percent in control of our happiness, but we can still control a great portion of it. In other words, it is up to us to spend that 40 percent in choices that will lead us to feeling good.

My happiness journey made me realize we don't need to wait for a big package, such as the purchase of a car or a job promotion, to be happier. Although those big packages contribute to our happiness, we can have small packages full of happiness delivered to us every single day. Small happiness packages are delivered to us through the *practice of*

---

102. Lyubomirsky, *The How of Happiness*, Chapter 1, The 40 Percent Solution section.

habits based on our principles and beliefs that match our own life expecta-tions. Again, it's up to us to make the choice of practicing such habits.

With all that said, I encourage you to create lasting positive chang-es through habits or rituals. As Ben-Shahar says, "If we want to enjoy lasting-change, we have to introduce rituals; otherwise the change is temporary and very often disappears."[103] To help you create lasting posi-tive changes through habits, I invite you to use the components of My Happiness Habit Journal.

Based on my own experience, after addressing the components of My Happiness Habit Journal for at least three weeks, I strongly believe you will

- develop more self-knowledge;
- identify what makes you happier;
- take responsibility for your happiness;
- better control your stress;
- feel more courageous, especially when facing challenging situations;
- live a more purposeful and mindful life; and
- create long-lasting happiness.

How to Use My Happiness Habit Journal

After sharing the idea of My Happiness Habit Journal with other peo-ple, I heard comments such as, "This is a great idea! But people may not have the time to fill out the journal or practice all those habits ev-ery day"; "People have to be disciplined to do that"; and "This would work only for disciplined people." My reaction to those comments? Yes, disciplined people would find it easier to incorporate all the thir-teen components of the journal in their everyday lives and stick to

---

103. Ben-Shahar, interview.

them. However, it doesn't take more than ten minutes to fill out the journal. Besides, when filling out the journal, people don't have to address all the components or perform all the habits to benefit from My Happiness Habit Journal. People should consider this journal as a menu of sources of happiness. They can choose the happiness sources that work for them.

My Happiness Habit Journal has the following thirteen components, which are based on what I have learned from happiness experts and my happiness journey:

1. Happiness-source goals
2. Gratitudes
3. Circle of life
4. Happy moments
5. A conscious struggle
6. My commandments
7. Resolutions
8. Tiny habits
9. An accomplishment
10. An act of kindness
11. Spiritual master
12. Overall day rating
13. Happiness Trophy

I agree that thirteen components can be overwhelming, but I should mention that you can combine some of them. For example, you can create a *tiny habit* to help you address a *resolution*. Say you have the *resolution* of *practicing the piano for fifteen minutes*. Then, your *tiny habit* can be, *"After I have dinner, I will practice the piano for fifteen minutes."* Or you can combine the *service goal* (from the circle of life) with *an act of kindness.* For instance, you can have, *"perform an act of kindness"* as your *service goal.* Combining the components will not only make the journal less overwhelming, but, most importantly, it also will reinforce the new habits.

I came up with three different ways to use My Happiness Habit Journal. I encourage you to choose the way that best fits you. You can also create your own way of using the journal; if you do it, please share it with me at myhappinesshabitjournal@outlook.com.

Here are my suggestions for how to use My Happiness Habit Journal:

- Use it as a menu of happiness sources, meaning that you can choose the source(s) you want to focus on. For example, if you want to focus on gratitude, only fill out the happiness source *gratitude* in the journal.

- Start implementing only one happiness source at a time and gradually add new happiness sources into your routine. For instance, in the first week, you can focus on performing *an act of kindness* in your daily routine. Then, three weeks later, you can add writing down two *happy moments* to your routine, and so on.

- Fill out the first two components of My Happiness Habit Journal (*happiness-source goals* and *gratitudes*) in the morning and the other ones at night. (This is how I use the journal.)

No matter how you use My Happiness Habit Journal, it is essential that you personalize the journal for *you.* Different things make different people happy. So create *tiny habits, resolutions, commandments, and circle-of-life goals* based on *your* values, what matters to *you*, and what makes *you* happy.

Components of My Happiness Habit Journal

Here I present each component of My Happiness Habit Journal by stating its *purpose*, explaining *what to do* to apply it, and providing *examples* to illustrate how it is used.

Part 1: To be filled out in the morning

1. Happiness-source goals

The happiness-source goals are subdivided into four goals: meaningful, pleasurable, challenging, and unpleasurable.

Pleasurable and meaningful happiness-source goals:

Purpose:

Encourage you to think of two good actions you plan to experience that day. Knowing that your brain does not distinguish reality from imagination, your thoughts anticipate similar good feelings that you will feel when you actually perform those actions.

What to do:

Identify one meaningful and one pleasurable action you plan to do that day. Since some actions can be meaningful and pleasurable, it is OK if these two happiness-source goals overlap.

Examples:

- Pleasurable goal: Watch the new season of *Gilmore Girls*.
- Meaningful goal: Answer my niece's text messages.
- Meaningful and pleasurable goal: Have lunch and talk with my friends Sergio and Katia.

Unpleasurable and challenging happiness-source goals:

Purpose:
Encourage you to shift your perspective on particular actions from negative to positive. In other words, when doing these tasks, you should not focus on the fact that you dislike them or that they are difficult tasks to be completed. Instead, you should focus on the idea that they are sources of happiness, since they will bring you good feelings in the end.

What to do:
Identify one unpleasurable and one challenging action you have to do that day. They should be actions that will bring you good feelings once they are completed. Since some actions can be challenging and unpleasurable, it is OK if your happiness-source goals for these two categories overlap.

Examples:

- Challenging goal: Prepare and deliver a speech.
- Unpleasurable goal: Clean the house.
- Challenging and unpleasurable goal: Study for the statistics exam.

2. Gratitudes

Purpose:
Create a positive mind by training your mind to search for good things. As a result of training your mind to scan for the good, you become a more optimistic person. For example, when faced with problems, your mind automatically looks for positive things, helping you make better decisions and see positive realities (than if your brain was functioning at a neutral or negative state).

What to do:

Think about the last twenty-four hours and write down three things for which you are grateful. The gratitudes can be small or big. Avoid repeating the same gratitudes from day to day in order to force your mind to search for more good things in your life.

Examples:

- I'm grateful for having a delicious salad for lunch.
- I'm grateful for talking with my nephews and niece.

Part II: To be filled out at night

3. Circle of life

The circle of life involves the following areas: *health, social, relationship with a significant other, family, spiritual, emotional, professional, financial, intellectual,* and *service.*

Purpose:

Encourage you to develop more self-knowledge in terms of how you can regularly address each area in the circle to bring you a more balanced and happier life.

What to do:

Create one or more small concrete goals for each area of the circle of life. You don't have to change your goals often, but you can if you wish. At the end of the day, check the areas of the circle of life that you addressed that day. You should only check the areas from which you performed at least one of the goals. For example, let's say that *exercise* and *eat a healthy snack* were two goals you set for the *health* area of life. On a particular day, you exercised but didn't eat a healthy snack. Although you didn't perform both goals, you still check the *health* area because you performed at least one of its goals.

Examples:

- *Health*—Eat a piece of fruit for a snack.
- *Social*—Send a text message to a friend.
- *Relationship with a significant other*—Compliment him or her.
- *Family*—Start a conversation with my family during dinner.
- *Spiritual*—Say a prayer before going to bed.
- *Emotional*—Meditate; fill out My Happiness Habit Journal.
- *Professional*—Create lesson plans; grade assignments.
- *Financial*—Keep track of my expenses; deposit twenty dollars in my savings account.
- *Intellectual*—Read a book; watch the news.
- *Service*—Compliment, help, or thank someone.

4. Happy moments

Purpose:
Encourage you to scan for your positive experiences, notice good things that happened to you, and identify your happiness boosters. Moreover, writing down two happy moments you had makes you relive those moments, bringing the same good feelings you felt when you experienced them.

What to do:
Write down two sentences to describe two happy moments you had during the day (one sentence for each happy moment).

Examples:

- Today I felt happy when I had a meaningful conversation with my friends Val and Shanna.
- Running into Theresa and Yvonne at the conference made me very happy today.

5. A conscious struggle

Purpose:
Help you realize what you need to better so that you can try to improve it in the following days.

What to do:
Write something you noticed that you want to improve in order to feel better about yourself.

Examples:

- Be more patient with others.
- Smile more.

6. My commandments

Purpose:
Encourage you to reflect on values and principles you want to practice in life and remind you to keep acting according to them.

What to do:
Create commandments, that is, principles you want for your life. You can create as many commandments as you wish.

Examples:

- Be confident.
- Be grateful.

7. Resolutions

Purpose:
Encourage you to practice new habits that will boost your happiness.

What to do:
In the beginning of each month, based on what can make you happier, create resolutions or new habits (no more than three) you would like to incorporate in your daily routine. At the end of the day, check the resolutions that you accomplished during the day. Once a new month begins, create new resolutions and carry out the ones from previous months.

Examples:

- Read for twenty minutes.
- Play the piano.

8. Tiny habits

Purpose:
Encourage you to practice new habits that will boost your happiness. This activity is very similar to the resolution one. The difference between tiny habits and resolutions is that the tiny habit involves a small habit (as the name suggests), and it is triggered by a habit you already have.

What to do:

In the beginning of each month, create new tiny habits (no more than three) that you would like to incorporate in your daily routine. Create the tiny habits by attaching them to habits you already have. Use the following sentence structure to create a new tiny habit: after I...(a habit you already have), I will...(the new tiny habit). At the end of the day, check the tiny habits that you accomplished during the day. Once a new month begins, if you want, create new tiny habits and carry out the previous month's tiny habits.

Examples:

- After I eat breakfast, I will write three things I am grateful for.
- After I exercise, I will meditate for five minutes.

9. An accomplishment

Purpose:

Bring you good feelings due to chemicals (e.g., dopamine) that accomplishments release into your body.

What to do:

Identify an accomplishment you had on that day. The accomplishment can be small or big, significant or insignificant.

Examples:

- I sent out all the thank-you cards.
- I submitted a manuscript to a journal.

10. An act of kindness

Purpose:
Make someone feel good and smile, and contribute to making the world a better place.

What to do:
Perform an act of kindness every day. The act of kindness can be to help, thank, or offer a genuine compliment to someone.

Examples:

- I helped Leily plan her week, and that made her feel less overwhelmed.
- I texted Melika to say that I really appreciated her feedback on my writing.

11. Spiritual master

Purpose:
Imitate your spiritual master in order to strengthen your attitudes and ways of thinking, especially when facing challenging situations.

What to do:
Select someone to be your spiritual master, that is, someone whose traits and attitudes you admire and would like to acquire. Your spiritual master can be anyone—famous or not, alive or not. It can be a saint, an actor or actress, a teacher, a writer, a family member, or a friend. Always keep your spiritual master in mind to serve you as an inspiration on how to act, think, and grow as a person.

Example:

- My grandmother is my spiritual master.

12. Overall day rating

Purpose:
Reflect on how you felt throughout the day. By doing so, you will get to know yourself better as to what actions and thoughts can lead you to positive, neutral, and negative feelings.

What to do:
Think about your day; then, rate it by drawing a happy, neutral, or sad face.

Example:

- ☺

13. Happiness Trophy

Purpose:
Relive the good moments you had during the week as you scan for the happiest one. Your mind doesn't distinguish reality from imagination. So when you relive happy moments, you again feel the good feelings you felt when you first experienced them.

What to do:
On Sunday, think about the good moments you had during the week. Identify the happiest moment; the Happiness Trophy goes to the person

with whom you spent that moment. Let that person know that you spent the happiest moment of your week with him or her.

Examples:

- "My happiest moment this week was when I got a new toy. So my Happiness Trophy goes to my father because I was with him. He was the one who took me to the store and gave me the toy." Vitor, my nephew, shared this with me when I asked to whom he would give his Happiness Trophy.
- One day I told my friend Diana, "My Happiness Trophy goes to you. Having a meaningful conversation with you was my happiest moment this week."

As I mentioned earlier, the purpose of My Happiness Habit Journal is to help you create happiness through positive habits that will bring you good feelings. You don't have to address all thirteen components of My Happiness Habit Journal every day. You should see them as a menu of happiness sources. You can choose the ones that work for you and then, if you want to, gradually add other components into your daily routine. The important thing is that you use My Happiness Habit Journal as a tool to help you take action to create happiness in your everyday life. Use it to help you make meaningful choices—of behavior, thoughts, words, and attitudes to boost *your* happiness.

I would love to hear from you. Feel free to contact me at myhappinesshabitjournal@outlook.com to send comments, suggestions, or questions on the book, including My Happiness Habit Journal. I'll be happy to help you personalize your journal based on what can make *you* have a happier life.

Afterword

At the end of spring 2016, I finished my happiness journey that I described in this book. Now it is the beginning of spring 2018, so here's an update on my life.

I became a PhD candidate. I am done with my graduate courses and assistantship, so I don't have to commute every week to College Station anymore. Texas A&M University offered me a teaching position, but I chose not to accept it, in order to focus on my dissertation so that I can graduate this summer.

Now that I have been working from home on my dissertation, I have to be very mindful about how I spend my time. Having said that, I have created a schedule that focuses on maintaining a work-life balance. That is, when creating my schedule, I made sure to include not only time for work, but also time for myself and for the people I care about. Therefore, my schedule includes everything that makes me happy: productivity at work, social connections, good habits, and relaxation.

I am getting up at six o'clock now, instead of five thirty or earlier. So I have been sleeping for at least seven hours every night, and some nights I get eight hours or more.

I have been cold-sore-free since I started my new-me journey.

I still FaceTime with my grandma, Uncle Fontenele, and Aunt Margareth every week. That's something I always look forward to. My grandma will be ninety-six years old next month, and she's doing very well. She's already thinking of her one hundredth birthday party. As for my uncle Fontelene, who was diagnosed with pancreatic cancer in 2013, he is fine. His cancer is stable, which several doctors cannot even explain.

Kent and I have created a monthly housework date. Instead of constantly nagging each other to do housework, we now do it together. We make a list of maintenance tasks needed for the house and tackle it on our monthly housework date.

I can't remember the last time when Kent asked me, "So what's your point?" It shows that my *be-clear* resolution is working.

I have included new habits into my routine, based on what gives me a sense of growth and makes me feel healthier. Learning Spanish, practicing the piano, and drinking more water are some of them.

One day I came across GoodThink (http://goodthinkinc.com), whose cofounder is Shawn Achor. GoodThink invites people to share their stories of how positive psychology has made a tangible difference in their lives. So I shared my story in the happiness archive on GoodThink (http://goodthinkinc.com/story). A few weeks later, I received an e-mail saying, "Shawn chose your story to share on his social pages Monday, August 22. Thank you for helping to spread the #rippleeffect!" On the day that my story was shared, almost two hundred people "liked" it, and several people shared it with their own Facebook friends.

I have joined the Better App, created by Gretchen Rubin. I recommend you join it too (https://www.betterapp.us). At the Better App, you can find a community that supports each other and focuses on positivity.

Professor Patricia Goodson invited me to be a POWER (Promoting Outstanding Writing for Excellence in Research) consultant at Texas A&M University. It's been very gratifying to support other graduate students in their writing projects.

I continue to feed my mind with happiness and topics that lead me to happiness—for example, productivity, health, mind, and habits. In this past year, I've learned from books such as *The Productivity Project,* by Chris Bailey; *The Power of Habit,* by Charles Duhigg; *You Are Not Your Brain,* by Jeffrey M. Schwartz and Rebecca Gladding; *11 habitos em 11 semanas* (11 Habits in 11 Weeks), by Dr. Icaro Alcantara; and *Positivity,* by Barbara Fredrickson. Now, I am looking forward to reading *Broadcasting Happiness,* by Michelle Gielan; *Big Potential,* by Shawn Achor; and *The Four Tendencies,* by Gretchen Rubin. Moreover, Brian Johnson's PhilosophersNotes (https://www.optimize.me/philosophers-notes) has been a great resource to optimize my personal growth, which, consequently, optimizes my happiness.

It's been great to share with you my new-me journey, which turned into my happiness journey. I hope my journey has inspired you to start or continue your journey where you focus your attention on creating your own lasting happiness through meaningful choices and habits.

About The Author

A ngelica Ribeiro holds a master's degree in multicultural education from the University of Massachusetts Amherst. She has worked with English learners and preservice teachers in the United States and Brazil for over seventeen years.

Currently a PhD candidate at Texas A&M University, Ribeiro studies curriculum and instruction with a focus on English as a second language. She hopes to one day work as a higher-education professor while helping others benefit from her happiness research. She lives in Houston, Texas.

Bibliography

Achor, Shawn. *Before Happiness: The 5 Hidden Keys to Achieving Success, Spreading Happiness, and Sustaining Positive Change.* New York: Crown Business, 2013.

Achor, Shawn. *Big Potential: How Transforming the Pursuit of Success Raises Our Achievement, Happiness, and Well-Being.* New York: Currency, 2018.

Achor, Shawn. *The Happiness Advantage: The Seven Principles that Fuel Success and Performance at Work.* New York: Virgin Books, 2011.

Achor, Shawn. "The Happy Secret to Better Work." Filmed May 2011 at TEDxBloomington, Bloomington IN. Video, 12:14. https://www.ted.com/talks/shawn_achor_the_happy_secret_to_better_work.

Achor, Shawn. "Shawn Achor on Happiness," interview, *Success Magazine.* YouTube video, 11:30. July 13, 2011. https://www.youtube.com/watch?v=8IdR76uegDg&app=desktop.

Alcantara, Icaro. *11 Habitos em 11 Semanas: O Guia Pratico para Seu Bem-Estar e uma Vida Plena* (11 Habits in 11 Weeks: A Method to Promote Health and Prevent Diseases). Sao Paulo: Companhia Editora Nacional, 2015.

Bailey, Chris. *The Productivity Project: Accomplishing More by Managing Your Time, Attention, and Energy.* New York: Crown Business, 2016.

Bennett, Jeremy. "The Amazing Power of Your Mind—A MUST SEE!" Published April 2013. YouTube video, 10:44. https://www.youtube.com/watch?v=cLqjK3ddSy0.

Bennett, Jeremy. *The Power of the Mind: How I Beat OCD*. St. John's, Canada: Flanker Press, 2010.

Ben-Shahar, Tal. *Choose the Life You Want: The Mindful Way to Happiness*. New York: The Experiment, 2012.

Ben-Shahar, Tal. *Happier: Learn the Secrets to Daily Joy and Lasting Fulfillment*. New York: McGraw-Hill, 2007.

Ben-Shahar, Tal. "Optimize Interview: Positive Psychology 101," interview by Brian Johnson, YouTube video, 44:45, *Optimize*, June 9, 2015, https://www.youtube.com/watch?v=jTT7mJCpVq0.

Better App. "Introducing the Better App from Gretchen Rubin." Accessed February 14, 2018. https://www.betterapp.us.

Branden, Nathaniel. *The Six Pillars of Self-Esteem: The Definitive Work on Self-Esteem by the Leading Pioneer in the Field*. New York: Bantam Books, 1994.

Cuddy, Amy. "Your Body Language May Shape Who You Are." Filmed June 2012 at TEDGlobal, Edinburgh, Scotland. Video, 20:56. https://www.ted.com/talks/amy_cuddy_your_body_language_shapes_who_you_are.

Duhigg, Charles. *The Power of Habit: Why We Do What We Do in Life and Business*. New York: Random House Trade Paperbacks, 2014.

Fredrickson, Barbara. *Positivity: Top-Notch Research Reveals the Upward Spiral That Will Change Your Life.* New York: Three Rivers Press, 2009.

Fiore, Neil. *The Now Habit: A Strategic Program for Overcoming Procrastination and Enjoying Guilt-Free Play.* New York: Jeremy P. Tarcher-Penguin, 1989.

Fogg, B. J. "Forget Big Change, Start With a Tiny Habit." Published December 2012 TEDxFremont, Fremont, CA. Video, 17:23. https://www.youtube.com/watch?v=AdKUJxjn-R8.

Gielan, Michelle. *Broadcasting Happiness: The Science of Igniting and Sustaining Positive Change.* Dallas: BenBella Books, 2015.

Gilbert, Daniel. *Stumbling on Happiness.* New York: Vintage Books, 2006.

Goodson, Patricia. *Becoming an Academic Writer: 50 Exercises for Paced, Productive, and Powerful Writing.* Thousand Oaks: Sage Publications, 2017.

GoodThink. "About." Accessed February 14, 2018. http://goodthinkinc.com.

Graham, Lauren. *Someday, Someday, Maybe: A Novel.* New York: Ballantine Books, 2013.

Hayes, Steven. "Happiness Is an Empty Promise." Published April 2012. YouTube video, 12:27. https://www.youtube.com/watch?v=I3OkPiUqyA4.

Kaplan, Janice. *The Gratitude Diaries: How a Year Looking on the Bright Side Can Transform Your Life*. New York: DUTTON—est. 1852, 2015.

Kogon, Kory, Adam Merrill, and Leena Rinne. *The 5 Choices: The Path to Extraordinary Productivity*. New York: Simon & Schuster, 2015.

Lyubomirsky, Sonja. *The How of Happiness: A New Approach to Getting the Life You Want*. New York: Penguin Books, 2007.

Optimize. "PhilosophersNotes." Accessed February 14, 2018. https://www.optimize.me/philosophersnotes.

Ratey, John. "Run, Jump, Learn! How Exercise Can Transform Our Schools." Published November 2012 TEDxManhattan Beach, Manhattan Beach, CA. Video, 10:43. https://www.youtube.com/watch?v=hBSVZdTQmDs.

Robbins, Tony. "Feed Your Mind." Published September 2016. YouTube, 4:48. https://www.youtube.com/watch?v=AW6Qn3GVPOM.

Robbins, Tony. "Tony Robbins The Secret of Happiness." Published September 2013. YouTube video, 37:12. https://www.youtube.com/watch?v=WPh6rLjsCp8.

Rubin, Gretchen. *Better Than Before: Why I Learned about Making and Breaking Habits—to Sleep More, Quit Sugar, Procrastinate Less, and Generally Build a Happier Life*. New York: Broadway Books, 2015.

Rubin, Gretchen. "Don't Worry, Be Happy Now: The Science and Philosophy of the Happiness Movement," interview by James

Fallows, *The Atlantic*. YouTube video, 49:00. Series: "The Atlantic Meets The Pacific," October 9, 2012. https://www.youtube.com/watch?v=-3hWBREH4LI.

Rubin, Gretchen. *The Four Tendencies: The Indispensable Personality Profiles That Reveal How to Make Your Life Better (and Other People's Lives Better, Too)*. New York: Harmony, 2017.

Rubin, Gretchen. "Gretchen Rubin's Quiz: The Four Tendencies." Accessed February 14, 2018. http://www.surveygizmo.com/s3/3163256/Gretchen-Rubin-s-Quiz-The-Four-Tendencies-Fall2016.

Rubin, Gretchen. *The Happiness Project: Or, Why I Spent a Year Trying to Sing in the Morning, Clean My Closets, Fight Right, Read Aristotle, and Generally Have More Fun*. New York: HarperCollins Publishers, 2009.

Rubin, Gretchen. "The ONE Thing for Mastering Your Habits," interview by Jay Papasan, *The One Thing*. YouTube video, 1:01:37. October 30, 2015. https://www.youtube.com/watch?v=NsQEgxEpoOw.

Schwartz, Jeffrey, and Rebecca Gladding. *You Are Not Your Brain: The 4-Step Solution for Changing Bad Habits, Ending Unhealthy Thinking, and Taking Control of Your Life*. New York: Penguin Group, 2011.

Taunay, Tauily. "Coaching: Explicação neurocientífica—O coach" (Coaching: Neuroscientific Explanation—The Coach), interview by Paulo Vieira, *Febracis Coaching*. YouTube video, 28:08. May 30, 2013. https://www.youtube.com/watch?v=p9-rlFbPwT8.

Tracy, Brian. *No Excuses!: The Power of Self-Discipline*. New York: Vanguard Press, 2010.

Vieira, Paulo. "28 videos para uma vida extraordinaria" (28 Videos for an Extraordinary Life). Published July 2014. YouTube video series. https://www.youtube.com/watch?v=z_R5LHBeR20&list=PLqhCb-FgTbjlQRZRZ0yIPIdJAdOY6q_UR.

Vieira, Paulo. "Coaching: Contagio social" (Coaching: Social Contagion). Published June 2013. YouTube video, 21:19. https://www.youtube.com/watch?v=d-Y3sB-8uO0.

Vieira, Paulo. "Coaching: Prosperidade de vida" (Coaching: Prosperity of Life). Published September 2013. YouTube video, 22:48. https://www.youtube.com/watch?v=nGu7obxmxI0.

Vieira, Paulo. "Coaching: Revisao dos conceitos" (Coaching: Review of the Concepts). Published June 2013. YouTube video, 22:39. https://www.youtube.com/watch?v=pJrMHod0CD4.

Vieira, Paulo. "Coaching: Validação e linha de Losada" (Coaching: Validation and Losada Line). Published September 2013. YouTube, 22:46. https://www.youtube.com/watch?v=Mv3Wa2_kuNE.

Vieira, Paulo. "Como estabelecer uma visão positiva de futuro" (How to Establish a Positive Vision of the Future). Published August 2014. YouTube video, 16:14. https://www.youtube.com/watch?v=ihAKPjhPWsc.

Vieira, Paulo. *O Poder da Acao: Faca sua vida ideal sair do papel* (The Power of Action: Make Your Ideal Life Come Off Paper). Sao Paulo: Editora Gente, 2015.

Vieira, Paulo. "Tem poder quem age!" (Those Who Act Have Power!). Published September 2014. YouTube video, 9:56. https://www.youtube.com/watch?v=utl2liCGGI8.

Waldinger, Robert. "What Makes a Good Life? Lessons from the Longest Study on Happiness." Filmed November 2015 at TEDxBeaconStreet, Brookline, MA. Video, 12:47. https://www.ted.com/talks/robert_waldinger_what_makes_a_good_life_lessons_from_the_longest_study_on_happiness.

Made in the USA
Middletown, DE
12 April 2018